SUBURBAN LONDON CINEMAS

GARY WHARTON

Sutton Publishing,
an imprint of The History Press
97 St George's Place, Cheltenham
Gloucestershire, GL50 3QB

First published 2008
Reprinted 2021
Copyright © Gary Wharton, 2008

British Library Cataloguing in Publication Data
A catalogue record for this book is available from the British Library.

ISBN 978-0-7509-4953-8

Typesetting and origination by
The History Press Limited.
Printed and bound in England by TJ Books Limited, Padstow, Cornwall.

Contents

Introduction	v
1. Ealing & Kensington	1
2. Finsbury Park	13
3. Kilburn & Maida Vale	17
4. Woodford & Highams Park	25
5. Shepherd's Bush	30
6. Tottenham	34
7. Stoke Newington	39
8. Stepney	45
9. Haringey & Wood Green	50
10. Southall	59
11. Notting Hill & Bayswater	61
12. Swiss Cottage	73
13. Brixton	76
14. Stratford	84
15. Tooting	87
16. Waltham Forest	92
17. East End Cinemas	108
18. Woolwich	117
Bibliography	121
Index of Cinemas	122

Introduction

When I first set out on the journey that this project turned out to be, I was often asked what it was that prompted the work. After all, it was said, cinemas without people are simply piles of bricks and mortar; what more could possibly be deemed of interest? My reply, more often than not, was to say that just as you really have to look closely to see beneath the beauty of the magician's slight-of-hand, so it is with cinemas. Their appearance can often offer a genuine sense of wonder, an attainable fantasy for which a smidgen of imagination is the only prerequisite.

Much has already been written about the larger West End picture houses, but these words are shared in the exploration of the more eclectic curios: the suburban gems which still glisten today; albeit in somewhat subdued light. Nonetheless, large or small, ruins or with alternative contemporary uses, derelict or pressing on as working cinemas, they still raise an eyebrow of any interested passer-by.

There were a great number of buildings of which there was the pleasure of deliberating over before including the ones found within; from Ealing's sparkling Avenue and ravishing Forum Cinemas, to the immensity of the Kilburn State, the crumbling, cobweb phantom formerly known as the Walthamstow Plaza and a glimpse of the total abandonment discovered in the Circle of the Forest Green Odeon Cinema.

This is a personal selection and the entries chosen were initially researched by myself, gladly trudging around the City searching, discovering, looking at and finally recording sights that will hopefully prove as enticing to you as they were to me. As is inevitably the case with such a vastness of information, inconsistencies occur when relating to dates and so forth (as they did during the course of my research and beyond) and all correspondence is welcomed. In the meantime, do go out and visit some of the theatres mentioned; it is a journey well worth undertaking.

Unless otherwise stated, all pictures are from the author's own collection.

Gary Wharton

1

Ealing & Kensington

The Avenue Cinema

Melodies of the past

I have to admit that my first glimpse of the Avenue Cinema proved to be one of disappointment. Instantly becoming known in the neighbourhood as 'Spanish City', due to its discernible architectural styling, its tired stuccoed, oblong façade retains its unusual detailing but struck me as ugly in an unusual way. The building has a perfect glazed tile cornice which does offer some hint as to the delights to be found within, though it is difficult for the visitor to project beyond the soiled white exterior. Plans have been proposed for its renovation in the coming months and so it is worthwhile to see more than an almost derelict looking veneer presently on view.

Firmly established on Northfields Avenue since opening on 5 September 1932, a different sight now greets the enthusiast from the adjacent Northfields tube station. The thoroughfare itself leads towards the west of Ealing, at which point the former West Ealing Kinema of 1913 (later the Cannon Cinema) appears, now as the tatty, twin-screened Gosai Cinema, specialising in playing the brightest Asian features. It is odd then to consider why the original owners of the Avenue, Walpole Hall Ltd, imagined that such an under-developed area should suddenly yield the necessary enthusiasm in local residents to warrant repeated visits. On this point, of course, it undoubtedly succeeded; however, a first glance inside does not exactly make this clear.

From the substantially spacious foyer entered into by passing through one of the double-panelled glass doors, its scale of construction is such that John Loran, a maintenance engineer at the Avenue, upon seeing the place in old photographs, felt it resembled an empty hall. John possessed a tremendous enthusiasm towards all matters relating to the building, so much so that I believe he would be living in the former in-house caretaker flat had it not been converted into an administrative space for the current proprietors – the Ealing Christian Centre. The group has a longstanding relationship with the locality and originally made an unsuccessful attempt to purchase the Avenue in 1985 after its tenure as a Coronet Cinema had concluded. The cinema had been a Coronet since November 1981 and had changed ownership once before, back in 1936 when the blossoming Odeon circuit took charge (reducing seating capacity sometime after to 1,100). The Christian centre was, however, able to bide its time until 1994 when a mortgage for the former picture house was obtained from the district council.

The Avenue Cinema, Ealing.

Cinema architect Cecil Masey designed the 1,536-seater theatre for H. Usher of Walpole Hall Ltd, itself a compact little company, including in its localized circuit the Ealing Broadway and Walpole Picture Theatre (demolished in 1981 but with its frontage saved and repositioned in nearby Bond street). Only after coughing up the admission price to the lady in the jazzy pay box (1s 6d or 2s for the circle and 7d or 9d for the stalls), would the allure of the place begin to enchant. Positioned immediately to the right, within the small reception, the quaint pay box has today somehow managed to survive throughout all the changes at the Avenue. It is debatable as to whether the manual *Automaticket* machine, hidden beneath a metallic desktop, has been used anytime in the twenty years since films were last commercially presented here. A desolate, worn looking velvet rope, now of no further use, can be found hanging silently behind the counter and could quite possibly be a relic from cinema days at the Avenue. An extra couple of boxes were added much later and are located to the right of the entrance, constructed by the Top Hat nightclub, in residence at the building from the late 1980s through to 1994. Also standing there once was a grandfather clock and presently, a fireplace has taken its place once more. Nearby is the figure of a bearded man casting his gaze towards his love, which was situated above the fireplace but was long ago insensitively replaced with a bulky thermometer. After chatting to people at the Avenue and exploring the surrounds, only then can one begin to hear the tale of the history of this remarkable building.

Top Hat made a succession of interior alterations to the space, whose structure was first listed in the early 1970s, involving the removal of auditorium cinema seating, adding the statutory supplementary fire exits, boxing-in some of the glass-panelled foyer doors, installing ballast railing in the circle area and constructing a bar in the foreground of the foyer (which remains unused). The setting of the bar actually does make spatial sense because the vestibule, even with this installation, is vast.

What is condonable is the leveling out of the circle flooring; again taking place during the building's nightclub years, altered at a vastly crippling financial cost. The authentic stepped floor is still underneath and fittingly enough the Christian centre would like to return the balcony to its former state, but due to practical rather than aesthetic reasoning. Visitors and parishioners to the centre find it difficult to read their Bibles up in the circle due to the inadequacies of the atmospheric, purpose-built cinema lighting. Indeed, the distribution of interior light played a distinct and significant part in evoking a mood; a soothing setting which was once engendered by four charming chandeliers, each requiring twenty-five 60-watt bulbs. I had the privilege of sharing the pleasure of the seductive ambience emanating from the lighting that warms the Avenue; from the foyer to the main auditorium, it takes only a few seconds to transform the developing mood by alerting the eye to the change in the contours of the theatre. The electrics in the circles are now fairly unreliable and sadly, the utilisation of the chandeliers is financially prohibitive, resulting in their use these days being rare, though at least they have been retained in some state of working order.

Remarkably, only two of the four bulbous chandeliers are actually visible from down in the auditorium and simply by coming up into the circle, all are magically revealed. A further curiosity at the Avenue can also be spotted from this position: a large emblem, centrally-located directly above the stage, consisting of a Scottish thistle and Irish harp insignia separated by a lion. It is an unsightly looking thing, and one possibility of its significance is as a cast representing Great Britain: This seems questionable because why would Wales have been neglected? Perhaps its placement is related more to Walpole Hall Ltd, rather than any broader, far reaching symbol.

Any decent sight lines have long since been destroyed and a black box disco lighting rig now brings an ugliness to the remodelled stage area beneath. In *Cinemas in Britain*, Richard Gray defines the inherent aura of the Avenue as an orchestration of 'psychological

Interior of the Avenue Cinema, 1999.

appeal and a cathartic effect', which beautifully summarizes the mystical language spoken there in Ealing. And while readily admitting to not being any kind of expert in cinema architecture, even I had to smile at a definition of the building given as 'semi-atmospheric'. I would, in fact, depict the Avenue as being wholly atmospheric in every sense. It is truly astonishing. Cinema patrons in the 1930s, when travelling to far-off places was only attainable through film fantasy, must have lapped it up in a decade that started with a great social and economical depression, only to ignite into the flames of a world war.

However, the most unusual aspect of the interior décor has to be the vast, billowing, pleated velvet fabric covering the entire circle ceiling. It has been deemed peculiar in that most *atmospheric* theatres, the Astoria in Finsbury Park for example, contained painted ceilings to reflect the skyline, but the Avenue is a different case altogether. The fabric is not thought to be the original 1930s creation, but even so, its presence cannot easily be ignored. Poking out from underneath the edges of the velvet cloaking on either side of the ceiling are the red-tiled roofs from the village scene created below.

The auditorium at the Avenue has no windows and was painted in green and yellow tones, but by the 1980s it was rendered a rich red. In mid-1999, its walls had been introduced to the softness and light of white. Glancing around, the visitor will soon

The Avenue Cinema, auditorium, 1999.

Interior detail of the Avenue Cinema, 1999.

notice the curved balcony configuration selected by Masey, which is an illustration of a typical signature found within his cinema work. Traditionally, it would have been a half or semi-circle formation but here it slithers like a snake and looks terrific. Nevertheless, if you were unfortunate enough to be seated at the end of a particular row upstairs, it resulted in providing a poor view of the flickering light in the distance. As a matter of fact, moving pictures are occasionally shown at the theatre, projected via an expensive video facility but containing an appropriately pious and child-friendly theme.

Downstairs in the vestibule, the chandelier theme is purposely continued, polished off with an additional collection of four golden grilles situated on either side of the hallway. Enhanced by independent internal lighting, each works to discreetly disguise the now-defunct heating system. A further two, much larger than those found here, are set on both sides of the stage in the auditorium. Bizarrely, these two hollow, giant-scaled, ornate ventilation grilles are large enough for a person to pass through and lead out to the adjacent car park at the rear of the theatre. Behind and beneath the reconstructed stage are a mass of claustrophobia-inducing rooms housing the cinema boiling system. Spookily, and rather sadly, an enquiry window buried deep down at stage left remains intact but frozen in a time forever lost. A hydraulic lift for the theatre organ, long removed, is another lasting reminder of the melodies of the past. A circus troupe took in a visit to the Avenue back in the 1930s and as part of their show, an elephant was featured live on stage. This caused great distress to the musicians seated in the nearby orchestra pit, not purely as a matter of animal welfare but due to the narrow and limited stage capacity.

Walking back to the first vestibule, its low-panelled ceiling attracts the eye upwards towards the nightclub bar facility which has already been detailed, as well as down two parallel flights of steps. These in turn take patrons into the lower and considerably smaller second vestibule before eventually flowing into the auditorium itself. Debate has raged among architectural historians and cinema enthusiasts as to whether or not Mr Masey was solely responsible for the prevailing design aesthetic at the Avenue. There is an almost obliterated plaque, coated in a multitude of paint and hidden outside the front of the building, which reads: Cecil Masey – Architect 1932. But was his work, as it has been advocated, complimented by the interior design originated by Theodore Komisarjevsky? It was not considered unconventional for cinema architects to have no further involvement with this aspect of their project and therefore, it is conceivable that Masey played no further part here. Or did he work in collaboration with Komisarjevsky or would he at the very least have been aware of the later contribution? Komisarjevsky has been cited as creating the Spanish-Moorish vivacity of the interior, which proved to be, like the man himself, wholly seductive.

Coming from a Russian theatrical background, he was a set designer and director of some repute and went on to create a succession of striking interior decors for the Granada Cinema circuit through to the end of the 1930s. Komisarjevsky devised, in conjunction with both Masey and another well-known picture house architect, George Coles, a number of theatres in Bexley (opened in 1938), Clapham Junction (opened in 1937), Tooting (opened in 1931) Walthamstow (opened in 1930), and Woolwich (opened in 1937). The obvious question to ask is, if he did devise the incredible Spanish city interior at Ealing, proving a propitious success, then what reason would there have been for it not being accredited to him? Cinema architecture author David Atwell offers the evidence that a drawing of the Avenue exterior was found among the Russian's papers after his death, and would therefore be a validation. Yet Komisarjevsky was a personal friend of Sidney Bernstein, the founder of the Granada circuit, and for well over a decade employed him as its interior designer. So was he simply showing an interest and merely offering a professional opinion? The exact answer will probably never come to light. Something that is categorically agreed is that Theodore Komisarjevsky is credited with inspiring a similarity in the stylistic interior found at the Avenue Cinema. Further evidence of his influence at the Avenue presents itself in two other Granada theatres, the first of the circuit which opened in Dover and the other at Walthamstow, east London, both of which subsume elements of the Moorish stylisation and have been acknowledged as his work.

The façade at the Avenue first combined a cream stucco and green base frontage with the six letters of the cinema name spelt out in the centre of the frieze work. Odeon would later use the same area to position its own lettering in a slightly larger form to compensate for the extra spacing. The building is not large in relation to some of the others that we will be visiting around London; only 40ft in height, but walking around its east side, its span becomes apparent. It is perhaps not as arousing in its style as some of others, but I nonetheless regard the theatre fondly, and certainly any cinema which had its own sweet shop out front (now in use as a collectable records store with appealing lighting design a clue to its original life) has to be highly regarded.

The foyer of the Avenue Cinema, Ealing, 1999.

The West Ealing Kinema

Welcome to . . .

After our introduction to the sparkling spectacle of the Avenue, we remain on Northfields Road but way up towards the west of Ealing, where the Gosai, originally the West Ealing Kinema, is the second picture house worthy of a visit.

Its appearance as approached from the rear, which curls around Matlock Lane, stands awkwardly within the gritty surrounds opposite Dean Gardens. Being vast in both height and breadth, first impressions of the lie-stoned Gosai Cinema are not enhanced by a meretricious corner entrance taking patrons to the ground floor snooker club or to the twin-screen cinema upstairs. This match-box shaped access point exhibits a joyous selection of Asian pictures on offer in a hodgepodge display board devoid of any elegant sense of theatrical showmanship. In its life as the Kinema, the building was capable of holding close to 15,000 people within a single screen auditorium that has now been lost due to various conversions in more recent years.

The cinema was devised by architect G. Percy Pratt and became Ealing's latest public amusement venue in the summer of 1913. After internal alterations, most likely consisting of various necessary improvements to maintain its position in a highly competitive market place, it reopened in 1928, after Mr Pratt had once again been called in to guide the project through to completion. By 1930, the Kinema had been renamed the Lido Cinema, with a capacity of 1,097 seats and possibly some time in the early part of this decade, the theatre was leased out to the Regent circuit company. In 1938, the building came under the guardianship of an independent company that continued to February 1965 when it closed as a working cinema, only to be replaced by a bingo club called Bellevue.

Rear view of the West Ealing Kinema.

West Ealing Kinema, currently the Gosai.

The original circle area is now home to the Gosai, a company with only this cinema under its wing, and divided up with 165 seats in the narrow Screen 1, with the same accommodated in the more appealing Screen 2, complete with a small stage space in front of the screen. A former manager of the old single screen house now employed at the Gosai observed that as the building stands today, it is unrecognizable to its past existence, displaced in 1965, when not even the latest James Bond adventure *From Russia with Love* (1963) could save it from closure. Bingo came calling at this time and would remain in the stalls of the former cinema even after the re-introduction of film presentations at the new Studios 1 & 2 in October 1971. The Cannon Cinema circuit, prevalent in the late 1980s, and a predecessor of the current owners, had a shot at running the place in late 1985 when the stalls had been converted into the new Ealing Snooker Club which, along with the Asian Cinema, has remained ever since. The cinema has recently been demolished.

The Forum Cinema

Love, life and laughter

After seeing the fatigued remains masquerading in the shape of the once-glorious West Ealing Kinema, we now take a right at the end of Northfields Avenue to where the wayfarer comes onto Uxbridge Road. This is the vicinity of the ravishing Forum Cinema, now enjoying life as a Virgin multi-screen house.

The Forum and the next entry, the Kensington (better known as the Odeon) are rarified examples of the best of British theatres: strong, understated and wholly refined in their detailing. Unlike many in the disparate but redundant suburban moving picture pageantry, the Forum and the Kensington, though constructed in separate decades (the former in 1926 and the latter in 1934), have both proven to be zealous survivors in the prevailing fickleness of the entertainment industry.

Launching itself on 23 April 1934, the 2,175-seater Ealing Forum is now marvelously preserved, although its interior has suffered due to partitioning in 1976 into a three screen venue. In contrast, the exterior of its north London compatriot in Kentish Town (which also opened in 1934) is, upon first observation, in a dire condition. Both houses came from the imagination of architect J. Stanley Beard and formed a part of the Forum Cinema chain created for Herbert A. Yapp. Yet the neglected façade of the Kentish Town Forum, itself hugely similar in looks to its Ealing sister, has an abandoned visage to its Highgate Road appearance. This is despite the fact that the building is now a successful concert venue for a broad range of acts and prior to that, was a ballroom.

All the while in Ealing, the cinema there has been consistently the home of the moving image for nearly ninety years. A first shift in management occurred in 1935 and significantly, it transferred to an ABC in 1961; continuing under the same shield until the mid-1980s when the Forum became the Cannon Uxbridge Road. It would embrace the mantle of an MGM Cinema as recently as 1993 just before its current appropriation by Virgin.

Closing its doors to the public, albeit temporarily in March 1975, the Forum was to lose its solitary screen days forever with the swift completion of tripling which was concluded by the end of June. Initial celluloid offerings had consisted of *The Towering Inferno* (1974) in the 764-seater Screen 1, *The Godfather Part II* (1974) was in the 417-seater Screen 2 and in the smallest of the three, a mere 210 seats in Screen 3, *The Passenger* was presented.

The Forum Cinema, Ealing.

The Kensington Cinema

'The effect of the great illuminated square is most arresting' (P.D. Hepworth)

Contained within the confines of cleanliness that is Kensington High Street, writer P.D. Hepworth evoked an atmosphere first felt back in 1926 when he commented, 'Isolated and well back of a broad expanse stands the great block of the façade, solid and arresting as the front of an Egyptian temple'. And during recent summer months, ice cream and drinks could be enjoyed in the immediate area in front of this wholly dignified building, giving it a relaxed and discernibly European vibe. Its multiplicity is also acknowledged by Mr Hepworth, who concludes, 'At night, the effect of the great illuminated square is most arresting . . . it proclaims itself a place of entertainment, it gives him [the patron] a glimpse of internal warmth and colour and invites him in'. Even the contemporary visitor, with or without an awareness of what has come to pass within the cinema, cannot fail to be satisfied by a first view of the imposing Aberdeen granite face of the Kensington Cinema.

The Odeon has set a ticket office on the right of the façade and to the left, an ice cream concession has slotted itself opposite either side of a main entrance which has been rendered nondescript. Upon entering the foyer, the cinema-goer is presented with a choice of films across half a dozen screens. Its authentic and imposing 9ft-tall entrance doors, two enormous bronze urns and original Kensington sign have gone missing. Coupled with the black and white marble mosaic paving once trodden over by eager film fans, much has been erased in the course of time at this Neo-Greco culmination.

The movie world has seen a great host of celebrated double-acts, from Laurel & Hardy to Fred & Ginger to Leathart & Grainger. This last team may not sound too familiar but the Kensington Cinema is an exciting chapter in the story of Julian R. Leathart and W.F. Grainger; a team regarded as one of the most significant cinema architects of their generation. And as the sugary 1920s made way for the embittered 1930s, the duo created several picture palaces and further enhanced their influential reputations within the industry. Just as important was the fact that Julian was capable of articulating the psychology of his profession which went far in forcing this type of architecture to be a worthy avenue in the world of creative construction. Their 2,300-seater Kensington Picture House, classical in presentation, with its own tea lounge and gallery, is recorded as being one of the earliest pre-war theatres to be built using a steel frame. Leathart was a strong believer in the fundamental consideration that cinemas should and could be built quickly and economically with a number of architectural considerations playing their part.

It was Leathart who had coined the phrase 'inside out' to describe the atmospheric cinemas in the ilk of the Astoria circuit, and he was an advocate in the architect taking full responsibility for the overall design of a building, down to its curtains and door fittings. He called it 'authentic ownership', and quoted in *Architecture & Building News* (20 April 1934), he expounded, 'So many [cinemas] are decorated by others that there are many decorative misfits as a result of this haphazard procedure'. Perhaps this work ethic explains why some five years after opening, Leathart dismissed the façade at the Kensington, going as far as wanting it cleared. But it is still worth looking through 1926 eyes at a structure categorized as succulently imposing. An onyx urn, not part of the architect's design décor, once stood in the centre of the entrance hall (where a ticket booth is presently located) and black and gold woodworking on the doors completed the sensuality of a jade green and

The Kensington Cinema.

ivory coloured ceiling. Below this, the gallery and tea lounge were found by way of a grand staircase complimented by a terrazzo floor finished in red and white. Before stepping into the main auditorium, patrons could have moved to the upper balcony over a red, green and black carpet, set off by a grey, orange and yellow coated ceiling which generated a hotel-like appearance to the area. Warm grey, silver and emerald helped to seal the affecting nature by embracing a 'plan of admirable simplicity' in what was one of the largest cinemas in the country.

With an auditorium now sub-divided to harbour six separate screens, how refreshing it must have been for patrons in the 1920s to be welcomed by amber red lightened by tones of warming grey with a lighting sensitivity enhanced in an orange wash. Red and mauve hanging lanterns, measuring 20ft in depth, would have been suspended from the ceiling on green and black shaded cords and tassels above a heavy orange-soaked carpet. A glance at the proscenium opening revealed a combination of red, orange, amber, green, blue and yellow, coming together to form quite a visual delight.

Within a building where adaptability had been imperative, it had been the home of a Red Cross store during the darkest days of the Second World War and the theatre suffered bomb damage in the summer of 1944 but was re-opened as a picture house very soon after, and became a fully established Odeon in 1946.

By 1976, the Odeon Cinema was able to facilitate 657, 301 and 193 people in its three screens after being constructed to hold 2,300 cinema-goers. By 1979, a fourth screen holding 234 seats was added and, as we march on through the next millennium, the Odeon currently has six screens on offer.

The 'great illuminated square' of the Kensington Cinema.

2
Finsbury Park

Finsbury Park Astoria

'Stars twinkle . . . the sun shines'

Two plaques are to be discovered on the immediate left and right-hand sides of the main thoroughfare into the United Church of the Kingdom of God, the elongated title for the bygone Finsbury Park Astoria Cinema. Above the proclamation of 'E.A. Stone Architects' and 'G & S Builders 1930', segments of rotten wood from the exterior canopy roof are contained by an unsightly, yet practical sheath of wire meshing to protect parishioners as they attend the various daily services.

The Astoria as it was, with its yellowing beige-tiled façade and familiar chocolate brown metal window frames, expose more than eight decades of erosion that the picture house has endured since its construction for the Paramount circuit was completed in September 1930. Cinemas were sprouting up all over the country at a rapid pace in that decade, and its architectural intent, or at least that of the 'super cinemas', was to reflect the onus of its proprietors in making an exterior singularly recognisable. The juggernaut-like narrowness of the Finsbury Park Astoria adheres partly to this ethos but not in a commendable sense. It is impossible to ignore its presence on Seven Sisters Road, being very close to the underground station. However, as with innumerable others, once you step inside the building itself, it really is vastly superior and a gratifying jolt from the disquiet. If a common professional view of the day was for the creative process to be preoccupied with forcing an 'economical and discreet emphasis', then the Astoria blows this point away.

Edward Albert Stone, born in 1880, was not in actuality a qualified architect but nonetheless, he is a recognizable name among cinema devotees, predominantly for his Astoria designs, all originated in the course of three years. His portfolio includes the former Warner Cinema in Leicester Square, the Maida Vale Picture House and Kilburn Grange (both opened in 1912). The Astoria buildings began with the unleashing of their theatre on Charing Cross Road in 1927, another in Brixton by 1929 and in a very busy 1930, Stone's Streatham High Road, Old Kent Road and Finsbury Park creations.

The Astoria Cinemas were absorbed into the Odeon circuit in November 1939, which, along with the Gaumont-British, was itself homogenized into the mighty J. Arthur Rank organisation by 1945. Yet in 1930, Tommy Sommerford and Ewan Barr, the interior design team responsible for the Finsbury Park Astoria, could have no such notion in mind when devising their sumptuous dream house interiors. Grouped in the

The Finsbury Park Astoria.

atmospherics classification, the creative solution for the Astoria was modelled along the ideals of the American pattern of theatre architecture, with inspiration from Egypt, Italy and Moorish Spain, concocted into a splendid, jaw-dropping extravaganza.

If we start off in the main foyer, after strolling through the small reception area and pass a second set of those familiar glass-panelled doors, what greets the guest causes a double take; a tiled fountain in the middle of the octagonal vestibule, with eight supporting mosaic pillars. Now devoid of its goldfish and water, the barren fount was once painted in a sombre green and gold and is overlooked by an angular balcony reached via a twin stairwell to the left and right. Just past the former water sculpture was a troupe of little booths attempting to entice patrons into purchasing chocolate, sweets and soft drinks for the accompanying film shows. Upstairs produces further gems, including the sensation of literally stepping into it. It really is a near-3D trip for the eyes; all that is necessary to travel is to simply look inside.

Indeed, the whole place is breathtaking; it draws the guest along on a journey to another place, time and region. And although its dimensions feel smaller than the scale of the Avenue Cinema in Ealing, the stimulation aroused at the Astoria is far superior: causing an enthusiastic motion sickness from turning your head in an attempt to absorb much of what is presented and suggested here.

It is regrettable that the United Church chooses not to allow much public access because the Finsbury Park Astoria is a veneration which needs to be experienced. The entire place seems to dwell in the realms of its creator's imagination and I certainly felt this after my visit. This was before I had the privilege of exploring the circle area on another occasion prior to which the cinema felt eerie, with the floodlit crudeness of contemporary spotlights subduing its authentic charm from the stalls. The circle, where a lot of seats are missing, is not in use by the church but may well be when attendances grow, at which time plans to utilize it will be reconsidered. It is here that the most striking visual seduction occurs, while the whole aura of the building confounds.

At present, a great deal of what was the picture house tea lounge, with solid gold-coated ceiling set off by a succession of inviting armchairs and tables, is now virtually deserted. Once more, the bar facility which I would presume was a dancehall or concert hall introduction (later uses for the building) is built into a wooden surround just alongside the circle entrance and is quite unlike the majority of such configurations, as it is not oblivious to the sensitive architectural balance of such a unique theatre as is the Astoria. The faded outlines of a number of large and expensive Baroque wall-mounted mirrors attached to the surrounding walls are the only indication, having allegedly been removed when the building was derelict some time after the Rainbow Theatre vacated the premises in the 1980s. Progressing into the circle by way of one of its mystical-patterned wooden doors (an appealing embellishment featured extensively in the interior décor here), one enjoys the best observation point in the entire cinema. 'Here', expressed the 1930 *Cinema Construction Journal*, 'stars twinkle or the sun shines, according to the will of the chief electrician', delightfully working in creating a 'perfect illusion'. Of course, the painted blue ceiling was predominant in most atmospheric theatres and worked by adding a further dimension to an already confounding environment. The melody of the place begins from the moment you step into the Finsbury Park Astoria and its crescendo grows until here, in the circle, a symphony of sound erupts.

The scene below is remarkable: mock houses sit in a little square above, and on each side of the stage there are even towels perched on the edge of balconies for the residents living within! It provides a sweepingly detailed visual treat simply brimming in ambience. The Astoria's twin-consoled Compton organ (one positioned in the orchestra pit and the other, a mobile device) is no longer here but the house that Stone built to disguise one of its chambers is.

The present owners are an organisation established worldwide but they appear uninterested in the appearance of the general vestibule and foyer, much of which has crumbling walls or ceiling plasterwork. In spite of this, the Grade II listed Astoria maintains a dignified presence, with potential wafting around the darkened halls. A generously-sized façade banner contains the broadly brush-stroked insignia of the Rainbow Theatre which is still there after all these years. The exterior was specifically structured as not to allow for the positioning of ill-conceived advertising hoardings (poster boards) and only the cinema name, in condensed neon capital letters shined on the canopy horizon at night.

The Astoria was a major London home for music gigs in the 1970s and '80s and a collage of posters advertising various long-forgotten concerts can be seen in the hallway leading towards the main stalls. As the Rainbow, it opened in November 1971 with a three-gig residency by The Who. The band played there a number of times after, as remarked guitarist Pete Townsend, 'you'll have to like it because there's no where else to play'. In the 1960s, Jimi Hendrix set fire to his guitar on stage there while the Rainbow is also fondly remembered for housing the Christmas shows performed by The Beatles. 'The Rainbow is to rock music what Bond street is to London's smarter tourist: never cheap, often nasty but, nevertheless, with a reputation for being the best', begins author Susan Hill in her novel *Breaking Glass*. 'But still', she continues, 'for a band to headline there means that they are at the very least extremely fashionable, sometimes very good, and quite often both'.

The auditorium has been repainted since that time, but what a treat it would have been to either perform on its relatively wide stage or to attend a show here back in those days. But what of its cinema life? There was a seating totality of 2,802 in 1930 and this figure would remain after the Finsbury Park Astoria was added to the Odeon circuit on 8 October 1970. Regrettably, the last popcorn to be trodden on came less than a year later when the picture house closed on 18 September 1971. Following the conclusion of moving pictures, moving feet, in the shape of the Sundown dancehall, was to be the next pretender, kicking off in November that same year. Closure came once more in March 1972. A further stab as a music venue resulted in this too failing due to a £180,000 restoration bill, bankrupting its last owners. Genesis played a jubilee concert in that same year which also saw the Astoria attain a Grade II listing, only to be followed by closure in January 1982.

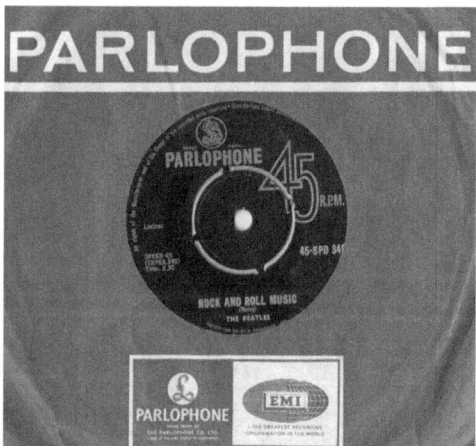

The Finsbury Park Astoria was used as a music venue in the 1970s and '80s.

3

Kilburn & Maida Vale

The Gaumont State Cinema

'This place of pleasure makes its bow to the world'

The most magical asset contained within the immensity of the Gaumont State (called the Kilburn State by most people) has to be the Wurlitzer organ; now nearly seventy years young. Specifically designed for such a picture palace, it is a beautiful piece of craftsmanship, symbolic of a picket-fenced America of the 1950s, strangely out-of-sync and delightfully antiquated. Around half a dozen recitals are performed each year and most are surprisingly well supported, predominantly by enthusiasts and older members of the locality. The Wurlitzer was initially positioned at stage-left but it is presently situated on the opposite side, after improvements were made to quicken the speed by which the notes are relayed through an electrical circuit. The reverberations that it emits are similar to that of water flowing down a sink; a coarse rhythmical tone gave me a slightly surreal feeling when I attended a recital there back in the late 1990s. There is most definitely a kind of funfair intonation reminiscent of carousel horses bobbing up and down, only with the back of the musician's head accompanied by the hum of the hefty pipes. I felt as if I was in a church but fortunately, without having to sing along to an accompanying hymn.

Its three sets of double, glass-panelled doors opening out onto Kilburn High Road were officially unlocked on 20 December 1937, followed by a combination of films and a stage show starring Gracie Fields and George Formby that evening, which was broadcast on BBC radio. A Gaumont British newsreel recorded the event for posterity, offering a brief description: 'Reach your seat with the least possible delay and trouble . . . in the maximum degree of comfort'. Facilitated by more than eighty staff, matinees cost 6s 9d for the stalls and a shilling for the circle seats. 'And so this palace of pleasure makes its bow to the world of entertainment' concluded the plumy- voice over, 'good luck Gaumont State'. Harry Hall and his orchestra continued to perform at the State all week. On opening day, the State became the largest seating capacity cinema in Europe with 4,004 seats, consequently generating a great deal of media interest, culminating with a newsreel being shot.

George Coles designed the theatre for the Hyams brothers who, crippled by the escalating £358,000 construction costs (compared to the Peckham Granada, for example, which cost a meagre £60,000), sought outside investment to complete the project and hence the Gaumont-British Picture Corporation bought a stake in the scheme. The original name was to be the Troxy Kilburn, a continuation of the Troxy name preceded by the Troxy Cinema in Stepney (see page 45). A compromise was reached and from its first day, the Gaumont State name was featured in all publicity materials. At least a thousand labourers were employed to work on the site, which took over two years to complete.

The justification for erecting a building on such an enormous scale and in an unfashionable area such as Kilburn was and still is, one of the brothers' explanation that the plot of land used for the State was the only one large enough and readily available to contain the new cinema. In actuality, the company could not find a spot nearer the West End than this one. Still, it was to be regarded as a further showcase for the Hyman Brothers Company and fortunately, what a roaring, Grade II-listed vanity piece it continues to be!

Cinema architect George Coles was responsible for the creation or reconstruction of the building's distinctive tower, housing a recording studio in its base, and like the Trocadero Cinema, it proved to be some legacy. His architectural drawings detail 2,648 & 1,356 seats in the stalls and balcony areas respectively. And after walking in, local patrons soon had the opportunity to muddy the marble floor (now sadly hidden away under superfluous carpeting). They would then have been (and duly are) welcomed by the lovely sight of a 125 lamp crystal chandelier, itself modelled after a similar design housed in a ballroom at Buckingham Palace, no less. 'If you like you can work out how often the manager has to put a shilling in the meter' commented a droll Gaumont newsreel at the opening. A second, rather smaller in scale, hangs in front of the twin marbled staircase, complemented by half a dozen little chandeliers arranged on either side of the inner vestibule.

These work well in giving a terrific contrast against the mirrored arches also found on both sides of the entrance. Fourteen, 25ft high black columns help in distinguishing the setting from being a replica location from the Orson Welles/Rita Heyworth picture *The Lady of Shanghai*: where paranoia abounded. (See the film on DVD and visit this theatre to see what I mean.) Due to its size, a palatial sensation evokes a 'city hall' impression with the visitor inclination of being in some way outside rather than in. There is truly a sense here of an eccentric, overblown pomposity shining decadently through its Italian renaissance, diluted to accommodate British sensitivity.

The Kilburn State is all about scale, made clear by its exterior canopy measuring a length of some 58ft. The stage combined a depth of more than 100ft with a height of 60ft. Not only that, but the safety curtain itself weighed 18 tons! More than a dozen dressing rooms were available to facilitate visiting musicians and performers. To control the stage lighting, a 14ft long control centre made up of 80,000 parts was required. Artistes as diverse as Bing Crosby, Frank Sinatra, Ella Fitzgerald and The Beatles all graced the boards here. Its vastness could be so overwhelming that comedy actor Ted Ray once bemoaned the difficulties incurred in projecting to a sprawling audience. This point is acutely justified upon standing up in the balcony and seeing just how far in the distance the stage is. It is little wonder that it might have been frustrating for those in the circle to be fully able to see and hear either the performers or screen stars below.

Upstairs there is a lounge bar, now in disuse, with heavy, dark wooden paneling all around that offers a strong contrast to the décor found in the general auditorium. Also located here, if you look properly, is a blocked-up entrance which led down to where cinema-goers to the 'Odeon 2' Cinema entered and exited (in what was once the restaurant area). The building is apparently fully intact due to a buyer not having been found after its closure as a cinema in the 1980s. A 250-seater Odeon was a 1960s idea, or a desperate attempt to plug a declining film audience, with the first phase consisting of two screens in the original circle and restaurant, coupled with bingo and a dance studio elsewhere. The late 1960s and early '70s saw the disintegration of the Kilburn State as a former house famous for its sense of occasion and impeccable service to a down-at-heart

The Gaumont State Cinema, Kilburn.

venue, no longer able to dwell upon its past glories. Audiences were almost non-existent, with television becoming the dominant force in the social habits of Britons and coupled with a poor, lacklustre film programming policy, the now 2,060-seater State was ironically living up to its title. Both cinema screens closed in the early 1980s but Screen 2 was reopened by the Odeon circuit in 1985. Around two years before, the whole auditorium had been refurbished for the sole purpose of bingo playing and the building's Grade III listing was promoted to Grade II. This meant that improvements to the State, which by now was in a very poor condition, were enforced and today 2,600 patrons regularly play in the single-level hall. Bingo had first visited around 1959 and after the theatre had been divided into two, a scheme, with the rear stalls used as a dance studio and the front stalls as a cinema, flopped. The present company policy is not to use the balcony seating and so it sits, gathering dust in the silence.

However, stepping out onto the balcony, the enthusiast is immediately transported back in time by four rows of dusty cinema seating with ashtrays attached to the back (remember them?) only to be brought back to the present by the sight of twenty or so other rows at the rear being blocked off, with the mere skeletal step foundations now remaining. There is a distinct softness to the circle, created by its lighting which is one of the building's most impressive facets. Especially appealing is the Art Deco tube lighting set up at the rear of the circle, now regrettably inaccessible. It would appear that the authentic State lighting fell into disuse in 1983; the vestibule chandeliers do still work but are expensive to maintain due to the considerable amount of personal care required to repeatedly replace bulbs and so forth. Those set out there are not as strongly affecting as the ones found at the Avenue Cinema (see page 1) but they do add to the structured atmosphere here and to other houses like the Avenue.

The importance that child audiences played in the success of cinema theatres across the country has always been a serious consideration for the many circuit owners since the advent of the 'Tuppeny rush' to the evolution of the Saturday children's shows. All have played their allotted role in providing a source of pleasure to generations of youngsters and the State Cinema is equally commendable. At the Bernstein Granada Cinemas, the grenadier clubs in 1928 were surpassed by the industry's acknowledgement of its youngsters and cemented in 1936 with Shirley Temple's acceptance as Honourable President of Gaumont-British clubs.

There was once a projectionist at the Kilburn State called Ernie Harry and it was he who came up with the idea of creating a Saturday morning show for children long before it became a staple of cinemas nationwide. Ernie passed on his thoughts to the management and voila! – the pandemonium, otherwise known as the kids' show, was born, to the antagonism of a thousand ushering staff up and down the country.

If youngsters revel in the collective enjoyment of being frightened in the security of an auditorium full of people feeling the same emotion, what then would they have made of the State's very own ghost? One female staff member had the shock of her life upon hearing the Wurlitzer crank itself into life in the midst of a deserted auditorium. She instantaneously ran out screaming. But what, you might be thinking, of the phantom musician? All will be explained shortly.

Many cinemas have their own story to tell about being haunted and a truly sad tale involved an escapologist at the Curzon Cinema, Turnpike Lane, who, in the process of his act would clamber up and over the ceiling rafters to reposition himself for the conclusion of the show; only one time he slipped and as a result of the fall, was killed. His spirit is said to remain, forever in turmoil and in search of personal absolution. But let us get back to the State Cinema where a shaken employee was relieved to discover that the source of her angst was actually the cinema cat scampering across the organ keys!

Music was of equal importance at the State, and as I have mentioned, there was a professional recording studio in the base of the Empire State-like tower. The BBC broadcast a great many concerts over the prevailing years but in a sign of the times, even 'Auntie Beeb' deserted, with the curtailment of all such presentations in 1977. Incredibly, the 1938 cost of the in-house sound and projection equipment, microphone and amplification system, totalled more than £23,000, a not inconsiderable sum now, let alone in pre-war days. There were two famous orchestras based here at differing times, the most prominent being led by Sidney Torch. He was the resident organist whose name is still highly regarded today, and his time at the State culminated in his composition of a selection of original material put down on record. A sixteen-piece orchestra was finally lost after the end of the Second World War, meaning that cutbacks would be inevitable at the picture palace. This affected staffing levels where forty or so remained employed, after its pre-war level had been an astounding 185. This figure was made up of various departments, including permanent staff, medical staff, cloakroom, ladies' room, technical support and projectionists, orchestra musicians and ushering staff.

The Kilburn State also produced its own magazine to promote forthcoming features to customers. After moving pictures ceased to entice local cinema-goers, its projectors were given to the Museum of the Moving Image on London's South Bank (now defunct). An original 16mm newsreel apparatus later found its way to the Odeon Muswell Hill.

Structural revisionism came often to the State and with the arrival of a dance studio in the rear stalls, there were serious repercussions to the general balance of the building. A level of interior alteration climaxed with the covering of original plasterwork designs, oddly to be replaced with a plain surface. Fortuitously, the work remains underneath, the positing of which can be found at the back of the auditorium, where the walls are plain, only for rich patterned walls to distinctly distinguish themselves as one walks down towards the stage.

The Odeon at the State Cinema utilized the rear entrance of the building via Willseden Lane, creating an impression of being an entirely separate construction. Its small redundant exterior with the 'Odeon Harlsden' sign is still there, only now it has been reversed, as is the case with vacant properties. Incidentally, this was the exit–entrance point which the less affluent cinema and concert-goers would use. The more well-off patrons would flow into the hall from the main High Street entrance.

With time, change often comes, and the floor at the State Cinema, along with the stage, were both victims of this transfiguration. The base of the auditorium was levelled off to accommodate the specific needs of bingo participants for whom a raked floor was not conducive. Whether there was an ulterior motive for this being carried out is not known but whatever the truth, the stage was affected and it was reduced to at least half its former depth. In addition, it has been boxed-in and occupied by a café bar and bingo display board at its rear. Gaming machines in the lobby leading into the auditorium with a flat roof replacing the barreled shaped one of the past, creates an anti-climax for the imagination before you even get into the main patron space. Thankfully enough, it is a pleasant surprise once you come into the hall and catch a look at the real essence of this marvelous building. The attractive gold leaf cornice is still here and its size gives a healthy indication of the immensity of the stage. The State struck me as a peculiar hall; what with its multiple changes and attempts to facilitate disparate elements (bingo, film, dancing and so forth) that never really gelled, even in its heyday.

I first thought about writing this book whilst on a passing train in the Kilburn area and caught sight of the red lettering spelling out STATE in bold capitals. This had to

Rear view of the Gaumont State Cinema.

be a cinema, or so I felt at the time. I had no indication then of the wonders contained within its lengthy history of enthralling audiences in the several passing decades that it has lived through. Whether you were a part of the Christmas pantomime audience singing along or you enjoyed the incandescent flicker projected onto its gigantic screen, the effect was always the same: captivation. Expansion of another more physical, or perhaps theatrical kind ambled through the State with the introduction of boxing and Saturday afternoon wrestling in the late 1960s and into the '70s. Famous names such as Mick McManus, Big Daddy and my favourite, Giant Haystacks, rebounded across television sets to the brief delight of a televisual audience watching the show on ITV's *World of Sport* show.

The cinema building is a striking place, with a domed-centred auditorium ceiling generating the dominant focus, while the elevation of the whole area is enthralling, even after repeated viewing. The State is included in the Open House access programme that takes place every year in London, the idea being that buildings of considerable interest (and not always accessible to the public) are opened for the perusal of anyone. If, for example, you would like to visit the Kilburn State to see some of what has already been outlined here, then you would be met with disappointment due to the fact that Mecca Bingo, the present proprietors, cannot officially allow non-members to be left alone in a gaming establishment. To become a Mecca member is free, but if you do not wish to join but would still enjoy seeing inside the complex, then I strongly recommend looking out for the next Open House programme. Failing that, go and enjoy one of the organ recitals which do not require bingo club membership. Otherwise it is just possible that you will miss out on casting your eyes on the giant, gold-painted organ grille work positioned on each side of the stage, which would be a shame.

Maida Vale Picture House

Pristine condition both inside and out

Within a few moments' walking distance of Kilburn High Road, you can find yourself in the comfortable confines of Maida Vale; along the way glancing up at the old Kilburn Empire (later the Essoldo Cinema and now partly used as a pub and gym) and momentarily pondering what it must have been like to visit such an inviting place, because it is number 140, on the Maida Vale itself, which we now wish to reach. It is here that the jewel in the crown of the district, the Palace Cinema (later the Maida Vale Picture House/Palace) can be found. Its salient green peaked domes make it an apt contemporary place for an Islamic centre, open to the public. Regrettably, the cinema building is now dwarfed by the hollow Regents Plaza Hotel and Telecom offices, but it is still a scrumptious, exotic slice of serenity.

Primarily, this Edward Stone-created delight will strike a joyful sense of misplaced recognition in the hearts and minds of all bucket and spade aficionados. Why? Because the Maida Vale Cinema creates an illusion of somehow being the archetype for classic sand castle molding used to create dream houses of another kind: those found on the beaches of many childhood seaside holidays. All that is missing are the flags of nations far and away, flapping in the breeze of years gone by. An insignia of another kind now billows above the north London skyline.

The Maida Vale Picture House.

Films began to be exhibited at the Maida Vale Picture House from 27 January 1913, when it officially opened under the control of Maida Vale Picture Palace Ltd as the Picture Palace. It was not only the Avenue Cinema in Ealing that hankered for an eccentrically refined touch, as patrons to the Maida Vale would be greeted by the sight of a grand Georgian mantelpiece after entering into the foyer across a marble floor. The admission charge was 6d or 2s, in addition to which local film fans could also enjoy the sounds of the T.M. Paiba-led, seven-piece orchestra, or sing-along with the cinema organist.

Around 1920, the cinema was taken over and managed by Provincial Cinematograph Theatres (PCT) and ownership of its lease changed again in 1921 and 1927. The 1920s was a time which found the cinema industry's need for the public was equated with people's desire for movies, resulting in more and more cinemas being constructed as demand steadily grew. It was not good news for local cinema-goers in 1927 when Associated Provincial Picture Palaces became the new owners of the Palace Cinema, by then known as the Maida Vale Picture House, increasing ticket prices to 8d and 3s. However, it was not all bad news, as the company did install a beautiful Wurlitzer organ upon commencement of trading and gave the whole place a fresh look.

This is a building which today finds itself in pristine condition both inside and out. Care has indeed been taken in preserving worthwhile architecture in the general area surrounding the cinema, with many other properties Grade II listed. Back in 1929, the Maida Vale came to be the latest acquisition in the PCT/APPH circuit of cinemas. I am not certain as to whether or not this is the same deal which involved the Gaumont-British Picture Corporation, but talkies would begin to be shown throughout the 1930s until the cinema's demise in the midst of the Second World War.

A primary cause cited for its closure as a cinema was due to the severity of the period. Still, by 1941 it had re-opened but as a restaurant only. Four years after the end of the war, the building continued to function as the Carlton Rooms Dancehall, a venture superseded by the installation of the Mecca Social club in 1961, said to be the first bingo hall in the country. An unprepossessing photograph of the new Mecca club features in *Cathedrals of the Movies*, a delightful book written by David Atwell.

Bingo made a second appearance in 1995, with the building undergoing a spell as Jasmine Bingo (the same company also occupying the Walthamstow Dominion Cinema). They continued in business alongside the Carlton Rooms, concluding in the early months of 1996. In the final months of 1998, The Islamic Centre England – London (ICEL) bought the palace outright from the local council and have since invested well in sustaining the elegance that this theatre has always possessed.

The Maida Vale Cinema was awarded a Grade II listing by the Department of the Environment in February 1991, which has preserved what was left of its original state. Little has been retained from its cinematic past, apart from golden plasterwork accoutrements in the main auditorium, which are accentuated by a number of attractive hexagonal clusters. Whether the new occupier removed the stalls or circle seating is debatable, but by the time ICEL took charge of the premises in 1998, no cinema seats remained. The upstairs circle is still there but the architect Edward Stone (who also designed the nearby Grange Cinema, presently a nightclub), would just about recognize his Maida Vale. It has been divided into two rooms and a glass shield runs along the entire length of the balcony. Asian films, some in 35mm, are sporadically shown as part of an annual festival for an invited audience of up to a thousand or so people. The video-projected pictures often suffer from audience members struggling to obtain a clear view of the screen. Row upon row of plastic seating causes difficulties, as they are obviously not stepped as in regular cinema fashion.

4

Woodford & Highams Park

The Majestic Cinema

Warm and cozy in our seats with our friends and a bag of sweets . . .

Woodford is an exceedingly pleasant locale, defying a village green description; it even has its own cricket green to firmly transpose the minds of contemporary visitors into the past. Directly behind the ABC Cinema (originally the Majestic) in George Lane was where the 600-seater South Woodford, later the Plaza Cinema, once stood.

This picture house commenced business around 1913, with a church as its next door neighbour, only to have its livelihood seriously compromised by the construction of the larger Majestic in 1934, right on its doorstep. The Woodford was modernised as a direct response to the threat posed by the new pretender and it reopened as the Plaza in September 1934, two months before the Majestic. The Plaza Cinema closed and was demolished in May 1977, whereby a Sainsbury's supermarket was built, incorporating the car park which belonged to the Majestic Cinema.

The Majestic's architect, S.B. Pritlove created the 1,724 capacity theatre which saw local MP and subsequent Prime Minister, Winston Churchill, inaugurate it on bonfire night, 1934. The cinema came endowed with a Compton organ to delight the ears of local picture-goers, as well as a ballroom and restaurant to please all. By August 1935, ownership of the building transferred to the ABC circuit under the new ABC Majestic tag. Life at the picture house carried on well into the 1970s, at which time its period as a single screen theatre concluded with the implementation of three screens by February 1973. EMI paid for the changes, although glancing around the foyer in more recent times, it is embarrassingly dated, with seemingly little investment made since the 1970s. It is a working cinema whose staff has been around longer than many of its proprietors.

Control of the cinema has passed through many hands, with little more than a half-dozen operators following W.E. Greenwood; for whose company, the Majestic Theatre Corporation, the palace was originally built. Next came ABC (a different company to the present one), EMI, Cannon, MGM, Virgin and lastly, the current proprietors, ABC. (ABC has around fifty cinemas nationwide, mainly garnered from Richard Branson's Virgin dalliance into the business in 1994. Virgin kept a hold of the more prominent screens and sold off the remainder, eventually selling its thirty-five strong chain in October 1999 for an estimated £215 million.)

When the Canon Company arrived in 1986, they had big plans to build a multiplex in Woodford by 1991, but such a scheme never saw the light of day and eventually the

The Majestic Cinema, Woodford.

circuit itself folded. After the Canon chain of cinemas was sold to MGM, the Canon sign was left up as MGM deemed it financially imprudent to spend a considerable amount of money on replacing the name at a lesser cinema venue, as this was considered to be. During the current ABC chapter, investment was put into the Majestic to spruce up the exterior façade, resulting in a fresh coat of paint being splashed over it in 1999. It is quite a decent sized theatre, and not at all loud in character; simply a little staid. With its ten, sturdily lined, glass-panel windows divided into five vertical panels, its frontage is crisp and solid. By 2007, Odeon was in charge of the building and had seven screens on offer.

The Regal Cinema

'The latest and most up-to-date electric animated pictures'. (1911 advertising slogan)

Just two stops from Walthamstow central station, Highams Park has a rural sensitivity with its foundations firmly rooted in the past. The Regal Cinema can be spotted as soon as you come out of the train station and walk around the corner onto Hale End Road. Opposite is where the Regal Café (now a mini-market) would have once sought to tempt cinema-goers into enjoying an ice cream after seeing the latest pictures across the way. The cinema building is still there but is now the location of a snooker club and weekend nightclub. Its chocolate brown brickwork retains its stateliness, as well as its cinema hoarding boards, positioned to the right of the main road entrance. Only one of a pair of flag-poles now stands awkwardly above, without grandeur, in a state of ragged abandonment. Vertical strips of brick give the exterior a sense of motion and the Regal name is now forlornly gazing down from atop of the main frontage. As is typical, a succession of disparate signage has littered the face of the building over the prevailing years since the cinema ceased to be operational.

Looking inside, there is virtually no indication of its previous life as a picture house. Regal snooker, open twenty-four hours a day, arrived around twenty years ago and a dozen full-scale snooker tables occupy what would have once been the main stalls, while bingo occupied the circle area prior to its current adaptation as a nightclub. Marring the interior is a false ceiling disguising what would have once been about 20ft of the general auditorium up to its original ceiling. How things have changed since!

'The most modern and luxurious theatre for miles around', as the original advertising slogan stated, started its life on April Fool's Day, 1911. The Highams Park Electric Theatre, as it was then named, was owned by its builder, O.H. Waitling, and from the detailed plans of W.A. Lewis, encompassed 550 seats. The cinema had its own 'Park' orchestra by 1913, where a modest programme was billed as offering 'The finest pictures. An ideal two hours entertainment'. Localised rivalry was projected in Walthamstow by the Prince's Pavilion (billed as 'the finest hall in Essex'), the Victoria Hall, Empire Cinema in Bell Corner, the King's Hall, Leyton, and the Walthamstow Palace, a variety house. In the 1920s, ownership was handed over a couple of times, resulting in the cinema being renamed the Regal by 1928. Structural alterations followed in the 1930s to keep the building modern, with the new Regal Cinema

The Regal Cinema, Highams Park.

A comedy favourite. Norman Wisdom's film *A Stitch in Time* was shown at the Regal on its release in 1963.

beginning its existence on 23 September 1935. This was after a part of the theatre had been totally rebuilt and the capacity was raised to 900 (though an increase of 615 from 550 seats has also been documented). A new organ was also installed and a café was added. In 1945, following the end of the Second World War, the Regal came under the guardianship of Norbert Theatres Ltd, and in 1963, Astoria Films (London) came to be the final owners. Cinemascope was introduced at the Regal during the Easter period of 1955 but due to its very small proscenium, the screen was simply masked off for the new format. Despite it being regarded as a very poor picture, *The Rains of Ranchipur* (1955) starring Hedy Lamarr and Richard Burton was the first feature presentation and succeeded in bringing people into the cinema.

Sadly, 11 September 1963 saw the screen fall into darkness, only for the building to reintroduce itself as the Vogue bingo club some three years later. Films and bingo stood archly, back-to-back, for the following year until February, when the Regal once more reverted to being primarily a cinema. *A Stitch in Time* (1963) starring Norman Wisdom was its first show. Meanwhile, bingo would carry on briefly each Friday evening. Bingo again came back on a part-time basis in 1968.

When interest in bingo started to tail off, a number of pinball machines were installed in the building and for a while proved very popular with local youth. The Regal would continue to entertain film-goers for a further seven years, when falling attendances made it unviable on a commercial level, whereupon it reverted into a bingo and snooker club.

Curiously enough, the Hale End Road side of the building is where most observers would regard the main entrance as having always being located, but this is incorrect. Two Regal snooker enthusiasts, Alan and Ron, now both in their early sixties, can vividly remember a side entrance into the cinema where a mass of children would be held behind a large iron gate, ready to stream in for a couple of hours of great fun.

Presently, entry into the snooker venue is by way of a side entrance and the nightclub uses the circle exit on the main road for its clientele. Weekly serials were especially popular with the young boys and girls here, just as everywhere, with Park favourites including *Superman* and *Dan Dare*. The Saturday morning children's show began at 10 a.m. and consisted of a 'cliff hanger' conclusion from the previous week's show, followed by the latest episode which inevitably ended with the hero in great peril. A selection of half a dozen cartoons was followed by a feature film and all of this was provided for the princely sum of sixpence for the stalls and a shilling for the circle. Rivals for the money in your pocket at that time came from the Doric Cinema in Chingford, others in Woodford and, predominantly, the Granada in Walthamstow, which had all the major flicks very soon after they had finished their initial run in the West End.

5

Shepherd's Bush

Shepherd's Bush Pavillion

'Imposing . . . with great imagination'

'Imposing . . . with great imagination' went the sentiment in awarding the 1923 special street architecture medal to Frank Verity for his design of the Shepherd's Bush Pavilion Cinema. Looking across at the vastness of the structure from the green, in a locality surrounded by perpetually congested roads and a past reputation for being decidedly rough, the Pavilion is awesome at first sight.

Verity was a well-held name in the business as a professional demonstratively capable of producing the goods, which was music to the ears of cinema proprietors whose concerns were often purely financial. 'I had difficulties by reason of the locality in which the building is placed', began Mr Verity, in acceptance of his award, 'The presence of the difficulties can, by thought and hard work, become the very road to an acknowledged success which has today been accorded me'.

Of course, the Pavilion as it now is, in the richness of Shepherd's Bush, shows a longstanding tradition for providing public entertainment. The famous trio consisting of the Pavilion, the Empire (now one of London's few remaining variety theatres and a popular music hall today), and Pyke's Cinematograph Theatre (see next entry) are lined up alongside each other in a hectic corner of the green.

The styling of the Pavilion was inspired by Verity's awareness and admiration of the 'splendid simplicity and beauty of brickwork' epitomised by Roman/Italian practitioners gone before. Nurtured during the course of his student education, this affinity would show itself in the resolution found for the Pavilion configuration. This was the commission that made his name in the business which had scant regard for the merits of the populist cinema architectural design. 'He could plan sensibly and beautifully', decreed Verity's 1937 obituary, 'combing masses harmoniously, he could decorate them consistently and gracefully. Work of his high standard is the fruit of a civilisation in which intellect and experience were held in high honour'.

The Pavilion, simply described as looking like one of those old fashioned, traditional box loaves of bread with an added Roman tiled roof at its far end, was designed from his Sackville Road practice. The adaptation of ferro-concrete for its incredible quadrant-shaped roof and the steel framework made the theatre a prime example of the modern 'super cinemas' to come. Its construction was swift, with the materials allowing a very wide span of space allocated without supporting pillars being necessary. Still, not all professional opinion was of this same calibre, for the Pavilion Cinema, author P. Morton Shand, was a little more taciturn. 'If not disclosing very interesting elevations . . . it is of the highest level of West End design'. The primary set of flag-poles and Pavilion name, attached to the barrelled roof, would both be removed in the years to come and an unsightly blue Mecca bingo corner canopy mars the entrance today. Its carefully crafted, rather austere flurries of exterior brickwork were worthy of merit and justified the architect's specialisation in cinema design in the latter part of his career. Verity's credentials are impressive, including a substantial portfolio supplemented by his advisory role as European designer for Paramount, for whom he created the Plaza Cinema in Regent Street and a number of picture houses in both England and Europe. This was a character for whom a succession of work showed his trademark of an 'urban style' which ran concurrently through his commissions.

Four stone pillars marked its flat corner entrance into which patrons would once flow, coming first into the vestibule and then towards a grand staircase taking them up past various rooms, allowing for the depositing of hats and coats or the possibility of having a nice cup of tea before or after the show. An auditorium plaque marked MCMXXII commemorates the official year that the Pavilion came into being and could be found in the sprawling 3,000-seater stalls. A total of 25,000 people were recorded as having visited each week back in the 1930s. How this must have delighted the initial proprietors, the Davis family, whose business also included their other two Pavilion halls at Highgate (opened in 1910) and Marble Arch (opened in 1914).

The cinema continued operating throughout the Second World War, despite heavy bombing to the theatre. In 1955, the Gaumont circuit became the latest owners of the building, continuing through to November 1962 when Odeon arrived, only to close the theatre in May 1969. It was split and divided into a cinema-bingo venue, with an 815-seater theatre ensconced in the former circle and re-titled Odeon 1. Robert Redford and Paul Newman were the masculine attractions in March 1970 as *Butch Cassidy and the Sundance Kid* (1969) marked its inauguration.

The Pavilion has had several uses in recent years. Bingo made its home on two levels right up until 2004, when there were muted plans for the Grade II building to be converted into housing or a nightclub. The coming of bingo would rarely prove to be a promising indication for the future of any working cinema, as all cinema owners realise. But this did not deter many picture houses across Britain attempting to cash in on the new 'fad' by actively utilising their dusty old auditoria on either a Sunday or mid-week, to intrigue punters with the offer of an inflated 'snowball' jackpot. When I visited, any sense of occasion or atmosphere was non-existent, since when you enter the building, its scale has been lost, and a sense of claustrophobia filled the air as any natural light quickly disappeared.

The 1980s was a decade which sounded the death knell of a great many cinemas in the UK and, regrettably, the Pavilion was one of its victims. The cinema section of the Odeon Pavilion faded away on 17 September 1983 and has not reappeared since, making a sequel seem unlikely. No seating or much else remains in the redundant Odeon 1, giving no indication of its heritage as it remains locked and abandoned

Pyke's Shepherd's Bush Cinematograph Theatre

'Clean and healthy entertainment'

A little Technicolour blob in a surrounding black and white world, Pyke's Shepherd's Bush Cinematograph Theatre (there's a name that flies of the tongue!) is dwarfed by the colossus of the Pavilion to its immediate left and the popular Empire music venue to its right. Though currently an Australasian watering hole, the Walkabout, it began its life very differently in the spring of 1910. Patrons of the pub today probably have little notion that the building was the latest diamond in the cluster of early picture houses owned and operated by Montagu A. Pyke, a monocle-wearing dandy, early theatre pioneer nicknamed 'the Napoleon of the film industry'.

It is doubtful that Mr Pyke would condone the contemporary goings-on in the rowdy environs of 57a and b Shepherd's Bush Green, as back in the early part of the previous century, he was not an admirer of that other popular social pastime; the music hall. Coincidentally, the Empire Theatre next to his cinema, upon opening, would go on to become one of the city's most loved variety theatres. But the raucous music hall reputation jarred with Pyke's ideology of 'clean and healthy entertainment; entirely free, not only from the indecent, but also from the suggestive in any form'. And like the great showmen of his ilk, humility did not feature in the make-up of Montagu Pyke. 'It will always be a source of pride and delight', he rationalised in his notes accompanying the opening of his Croydon Cinema in 1910, 'that I was privileged to be the pioneer of the picture house . . . I have done something to brighten the lives of great masses of people, to bring a little sunshine and happiness to them'. He then adds: 'I feel, however, that my work in this direction is not yet completed. I shall not rest satisfied until I have erected a Pyke Theatre in every London suburb and provincial town in which it seems to me

Pyke's Shepherd's Bush Cinematograph Theatre.

that one is needed'. He had many cinemas under his wing with which to implement such naiveté, including a picture house in Edgware Road, Finsbury Park, Hammersmith, Charing Cross Road and one we will visit later in this book, in Brixton.

Pyke's Theatre in Shepherd's Bush is an oasis in a desert, a little flag billowing in the breeze of long hot summers forever remembered. It is by traipsing along the alleyway in Rockwood Place (literally next to the Empire) that a clear declaration is found: 'Cinematograph Theatre continuous performance seats 1/-, 6d & 3d'. Cut into stone and using crisp capital letters, the sign proceeds down a good part of the structure. The visitor can see and feel its presence by catching a glimpse of Mr Montagu's yellow vision monocle to a non-existent future manifesting itself in a tricolour commemorating a revolution in an industry whose reverberation has long since faded around here.

Upgraded to the new Pavilion in November 1923 after reconstruction work to the order of J. Stanley Beard had been completed, this gives a key clue in explaining its longevity and adaptability. Pyke passed away in 1935, some twelve years after the Frank Verity-created Pavilion had cast its substantial shadow over Pyke's little hall. But his building has at least stood the test of time: it became an Essoldo Cinema in June 1955 but was struck by closure in 1968 when further modernisation was interrupted by a fire, leading to a delay in its reopening until the following June. A 500-seater cinema ran on throughout the psychedelic '60s before becoming the Classic Cinema in April 1972. The Odeon circuit took control of the theatre in April of the following year (with a restricted seating capacity of 487), synchronising well with the installation of Odeon 1 at the next door Pavilion. The end of its moving picture life came on 17 October 1981, with a double bill of *Alien* (1979) and *The Fog* (1979), after which the building became derelict until the future arrival of the Antipodean pub.

Pyke's Cinematograph Theatre, like its name, is a museum piece for a cinematic past. It proves to be a curiously eerie pilgrimage and succinctly sums up the local environment: a quirky smile in the aesthetic aridity that is Shepherd's Bush.

Alleyway in Rockwood Place showing ticket prices for Pyke's Cinematograph Theatre.

6

Tottenham

A diverting district where the Art Nouveau instilled delights of St Mark's Methodist church immediately seize your attention as it sits along the bustling High Road next to Bruce Grove train station. While in the colourful area of N17, we shall stop to take in five separate sites in advance of moving further north.

The Palace Theatre and the Canadian Cinema Theatre

'Tottenham Palace. Theatre of Varieties.' (Newspaper advert in the Tottenham Herald, *1908)*

At first beginning as a music hall on 31 August 1908, the Palace is a yellow stoned building that has maintained its grace in the decades which followed. Currently known as the Palace cathedral, it was adopted by yet another religious organisation in the late 1990s as its home. Bizarrely, this grand theatre was the only such house in London not to have been awarded a statutory grade listing for many years.

The creators of its construction have literally acknowledged their own work in a number of parts of its exterior, going as far as an engraved stone (located on the immediate right of the front entrance) reading 'Wylson Long Architect & A.J. Bateman Builders'. This is in addition to '1908' being found within the architectural design along with 'WL' lettering elsewhere. The architects responsible for the Palace also conceived the styling of the Empress Theatre, (later the Granada following reconstruction work and now demolished), on Brixton's Brighton Terrace.

Tram cars passing up and down the High Road had a new stop added to their routes with the opening of the Palace on 31 August 1908. It began its time as a variety house the year before, possibly under another name. United Variety Syndicate Ltd operated the theatre with an auditorium of the two-tier type. On the ground floor, entered by way of a vestibule dressed in French Renaissance style, close to 1,000 patrons could be squeezed into the stalls and pit, while 500 seats were made available in the balcony (though a total number of 1,783 seats has also been recorded).

A colour scheme of gold and cream with green marble pilasters and high panelled walls covered by polished oak combined to compliment a grandiose theatre set off by a white and green marble mosaic floor. The auditorium featured dark crimson-toned carpets in an area entirely fitted with an electrical lighting system, as gas was no longer permitted for safety reasons. Two shows each evening, at 6.40 p.m. and 9 p.m saw punters paying 3*d* for the gallery, 6*d* for the pit, 1*s* for the balcony and 1*s* 6*d* or 2*s* for the remaining stall seats. Research has indicated that the building was open as the people's Palace Cinema in 1907, but this contradicts somewhat with the 1908 signage.

Whatever the actuality, the Palace is an imposingly-scaled structure with its entrance hall and exterior looking more like a municipal hall than one for amusement. Its sprawling façade makes a feature out of the two windows opening out onto a small balcony and a much larger space above the main entry point balances five additional windows, which come out onto a veranda.

It would seem that the Palace had a change of name in 1911 along with the Canadian Cinema next door (itself called the Canadian Skating Rink). Constructed in 1909, the roller- skating rink became inextricably linked with the Palace due to the fact that both were owned by the same company at that time. The rink had its 'Canadian Rink' title up in light bulbs to entice evening patrons into a part of the complex that looked entirely separate from the larger, more prominent Palace and by 1911, both were featured in local newspaper advertisements. Even today, in the form of the Temple nightclub, the original site proves a prominent feature.

Further issues arose when interest in roller skating lapsed, and in 1913, the Canadian Cinema Theatre introduced some stability at the venue and continued through to 1926. At the commencement of that year, the Tottenham Palace offered revues and live shows while its neighbour, the Canadian Rink Cinema (CRC), presented films. Each entertainment house now advertised separately in the press up until September 1926, when the CRC re-emerged as the Canadian Cinema, with the cessation of live shows.

The Palace Theatre, Tottenham.

Confoundingly, newspaper adverts for the pseudo-exotic Tottenham *Palais de danse* would commence in 1925, only for it to have disappeared in favour of the singular Tottenham Palace Cinema in January of the following year.

If the building was constantly adapting to the changing tastes of the local population, films finally turned out to have the strongest grip at the Palace and the theatre consequently showed moving pictures for the next forty-three years. Meanwhile, the former roller rink/cinema jigged its final steps as a dancehall and then as a social club called the Ritzy around 1950. It did not, however, follow through this period without further disorder; a fire in 1960 caused a serious amount of damage to the Palace and closure was the only option prior to its eventual reopening at Christmas 1962.

The Palace's defiant attempts at struggling to make ends meet were finally curtailed with its closure on Saturday 28 June 1969. The building reopened later that year as a Mecca bingo hall. Local residents had already been given a taster of bingo back in 1961 and up until its own demise, the Palace had put on a weekly session of the numbers game. A Mecca Bingo spokesman interviewed by the *Tottenham Herald* conceded, 'If J. Arthur Rank cannot make a go of it then nobody can'. Despite this, Mecca, which already owned what was probably the former rink, then the Royal Dancehall, saw a decent enough potential in the Palace and far reaching development plans were voiced.

In the late 1990s, the building had two individual uses; the Palace cathedral in the main heart of the structure and as the Temple nightclub, its heavily themed exterior making it seem more in place at a theme park than in Tottenham.

The Bruce Grove Cinema

The theatre with no name . . .

Of all the cinemas in and around Tottenham, this is the most easily recognizable as one, simply by looking up at its home on Bruce Grove, as it rolls down towards the British Rail station in the direction that soon arrives in the heart of the main High Street. The primary shape of its structure is almost as identifiable as it was back on the night of 14 July 1921 with the premier of *The Mark of Zorro* setting the scene for a prosperous forty-two year period as functioning theatre.

Its architect is unknown, which proves to be a further anomaly in the life of a building that was known plainly as the 'Cinema' for a considerable time before its ordination as the Bruce Grove in 1948. Subsequent reconstruction plans carried out in the name of Robert Cromie in August/September 1933 are the only documented clarifications. Bingo and snooker each took on the mantle of the picture house, following the closure of the cinema at the end of August 1963 with a double-header of *Tamahine* and *To Have and to Hold* concluding its movie life.

The subdivision of the bygone cinema has now created multiple uses in its space, enabling the commercial endeavors of a pool club, a computer retailer, jeweller and video shop to co-exist, as well as providing headquarters for the Freedom's Ark church. The group has appropriated what was probably the main entrance of the theatre within a plain brickwork front with a veil of white paint. Common in its day, it was constructed with the longest length of shell providing access in and out of the building rather than the equally seen corner entrance used for other modern or 'super cinemas' in the era.

The Bruce Grove Cinema, Tottenham.

Understandably lacking in unanimity, the roadside body of the Bruce Grove is now coated in an assembly of colours all dramatically clashing. It is only the main access point of the façade that is of interest, where '1921' can be seen high above the towered entrance. The far end of the theatre is presently the location of The Edge snooker and American pool hall in what is believed to have been the original cinema exit, but which is being used as their entry point. The other end of the building finds the Bruce Grove video shop perched on the corner next to the church group thoroughfare. (One is denied entry by an intercom system but a staircase and a doorway presumably leading into the main auditorium can be seen.) Underneath, a curved canopy, once a mass of light-bulbs helped by additional strips of neon, worked in beautifying the curves of the cinema each night. None, alas, remain in any kind of working order and the picture house today pales in comparison to its heyday.

Bruce Grove Studios 5,6,7,8

Twice nightly . . .

Built in what was originally the dancehall attached to the Bruce Grove Cinema, Studios 5–8 commenced flickering images in the summer of 1974 and had waned by December 1981. Following a subsequent conversion to a banqueting suite, the premises are now home to the exceedingly spruce-looking Regency suite, shops and bank.

A mere step or two from the Grove, this is the type of structure that immediately makes the curious passer-by stop and ponder its past history. Its short-lived cinematic heartbeat provides the best of the brief spells of N17 picture palaces among others such as the Corner Cinema on Seven Sisters Corner, Stamford Hill (opened in 1911 and closed in 1960 prior to bingo conversion and demolition); the Perfect Picture House in Tottenham Lane (later the Plaza Picture House); the neighbouring trio of Palais de Luxe (around 1964 and later demolished), the Palladium (lost within a 1937 Marks & Spencer expansion) and the Grand Cinema in Turnpike Lane which shut in 1934 and was later used as a tea room, all of which have been erased.

The Imperial Cinema

Where the people have long since gone . . .

If The Beatles had their yellow submarine, then the resident of N17 had the Imperial, the concluding picture theatre of this itinerary before jumping on a bus towards Turnpike Lane and Wood Green. Situated at 290–294 West Green Road, it is recognizable by its three port-holed exterior windows, the prevailing characteristic in this crisp, almost nautical façade brought forth by architect E.A. Thorne.

Silent pictures began to enthrall patrons in this 550 capacity theatre on 6 November 1913, and in the intervening years before the ascendancy of the robust Essoldo Cinema form the embers of the former Imperial in 1949. Films finally ground to a halt in 1958 with *Witness for the Prosecution* (1957), and *Betrayal* (1958) being the final shown.

The building thereafter became a general store and, much later, the home of the Discount Carpet Co., ahead of the building's structural decline. At the time of writing, one of its two West Green Road windows has been smashed, marring an otherwise pleasing decorative frontage, embellished with brass work around the two lower windows (with a third forming a pyramid alignment), coarsely illustrative of the state of neglect that the grizzled old theatre now dwells in. A tiny metal shuttered entrance, complete with the carpet store sign above, rounds off its present dilapidated and subdued condition.

7

Stoke Newington

What an intriguing area for the cinema enthusiast; plenty to discover, if only a little out of the way to get to. Stoke Newington High Street, reached by a number 106 bus from Finsbury Park tube station, is the place from which our journey will start and where we can find five picture houses of some description or another, either in use or defunct.

The Vogue Cinema

A small cinema . . .

Directly across from the police station is the lonesome shadow of the Majestic Cinema, from 1946 onwards the Vogue Cinema. There is not a great deal to explore as the building is closed-up, but it has retained its signage, with the Vogue name in faded red capitals running vertically down its corner entrance. It was also known as the Vogue Continental Cinema in the early 1960s, the evidence of this being the heavily corroded Continental denotation currently decaying alongside its other remaining signage.

Today the façade is not much to look at, but it is interesting nonetheless. Its past existence, where once its function would have been to draw the public in, has faded back into the row of flats and shopping outlets running nearest its High Street side. The smallness of the building gives the feeling that if you were not actually looking to discover a cinema, then it would fail to register in the mind of either a seasoned local or a passing stranger. This could surely be a truism for old cinema buildings in general, now harshly adrift in an ocean of yesteryear.

The Vogue is a plain, pillared picture house which emanates an impression of being a typical corner shop from the past, with an exterior now little more than a ruin, its brickwork is exposed as a result of fallen, crumbling plaster corsetry. Exit doors located to the side of neighbouring Batley Road show a warped tiredness confirming the view that the building has not been functioning in any way for some time. Indeed, the Vogue Cinema fell into disuse as a film venue in the summer of 1958; 21 June being its final working day. Both films and stage shows had previously been presented there in 1954.

The Vogue Cinema, Stoke Newington.

The Apollo Cinema

Visually stunning...

Heading a bit further along the High Street, on the other side of the road, we arrive at the second and probably most visually stunning of the group: the grey-stoned Apollo. Back in August 1933 this was a 1,080-seater cinema, beginning its extended career as the Apollo and continuing to entertain locals till 1946, when the Ambassador Cinema took on its baton.

By the conclusion of 1963, the screen at this picture house would submerge into darkness for over a decade. Films returned one more time in September 1974 after the lights of the new Astra Cinema dazzled the few bingo players away, and would continue flickering until its demise in July 1983.

No clues emerge to detail the rich cinematographic days of the place, as the building is now employed as the Azizye mosque, with an accompanying restaurant.

The Coliseum

Look through the half circular windows...

Following on from the Astra and once again situated on Stoke Newington Road (a roadway that is a continuation of the High Street), is the Coliseum, or at least the skeletal remains that could once upon a time house 600 patrons but now find themselves partially hidden by advertising hoardings. At the top of its face, the Coliseum name has all but been eradicated, and when I visited, all that was left was a solitary 'M'. Its opening has not been widely documented but its closure as a cinema was in February 1972 with the Michael Caine drama *Too Late the Hero* (1967) coupled with *Hell in the Pacific* (1969).

The Coliseum, like the Vogue on the High Street, looks like a complete ruin. It quite probably is beyond saving but its classic façade, with half-circular windows above what would have been its centralised main entrance is a visually rewarding treat to discover.

The Apollo Cinema, Stoke Newington.

The Coliseum, Stoke Newington.

The Savoy Cinema

A remarkable story...

Still on the same road, at the corner of Trumans Road, the penultimate movie house in the vicinity is the Savoy Cinema. Six or seven individual business outlets are each housed in separate parts of the interior of the former 'super cinema'. Architect W.R. Glen devised this 1,800-seater venue which opened its doors on 26 October 1936 in the year that followed the addition of 150 cinemas in Britain. ABC took the building under its sturdy wing in 1962, though the cinema ceased trading by March 1977. This was not the final reel in a remarkable story that played on a little further. The old Savoy came back in the guise of the Konak Cinema in June 1982 through to February 1985, when not even the sterling performance of Al Pacino in *Scarface* (1983) could save the cinema from closure.

The Snooker Lovers Club was the first to go back into the discarded cinema building where it remains still. Another advertising hoarding, in keeping with the local council's insensitivity, cloaks the centralised heart of the concrete tower exterior of the comely cinema.

Rio Cinema

'The Rio continues...'

According to the Rio Cinema website, 'While all the other cinemas in Hackney have disappeared or become snooker halls and car auction rooms, the Rio continues to adapt

The Savoy Cinema building, as seen in 1999.

Rio Cinema, Stoke Newington.

Interior of the Rio Cinema.

and flourish'. The Rio Cinema, at 107 Kingsland High Street, Dalston, has proven to be a real success story as a working cinema in the heart of the local community.

Despite all the changing peaks in cinema-going over the years, the 400-seat Rio, a single-screen theatre, has prevailed. Dating back to 1909, the cinema plays a mix of art house and mainstream releases. The Rio concludes our visit to this area.

8

Stepney

The Troxy Cinema

'An astounding house of entertainment'. (Troxy sign positioned outside the building prior to opening)

Opening on 11 September 1933, its name being a fusion of two other existing cinemas in the Hyams and Gale Superior Cinemas circuit; namely the Trocadero, Elephant & Castle (opened in 1930) and the Trocette in Stepney (opened in 1929), the Troxy Cinema instantly became East London's largest and best known picture house.

Created by the prolific East End-born George Coles with Percy Adams, the Troxy, found on Commercial Road, stood directly next to another Coles' creation, the Popular Cinema (opened in 1913, demolished in 1960) and a much smaller theatre known affectionately as the old 'penny whistle'. Coles was reaching the peak of his creativity as the decade progressed, being responsible for other cinemas in the East End, namely the Savoy at Leyton (opened in 1928), the Rex at Stratford, the Carlton at Upton Park (opened in 1928) and the Rivoli in nearby Whitechapel, and culminating with the 1937 opening of the literally towering Gaumont State (see page 17).

Much has been made of the considerable amount of raw material needed to build the Troxy, which took more than a year to construct, including a total of 2.5 million bricks, some 24,000 tons of ballast (the coarse stone used for foundations), sand totaling some 10,000 tons with 1,000 light-bulbs connected by 5,000yds of wiring. The Troxy proved to be a reliable player in the H&G circuit, being just as impressive in scale, décor and overall aesthetics as any of them. It was considered to be just that little bit extra special, giving its customers the best quality features within a 3,250-seater auditorium seductively sprayed with a gentle perfume. During the interval on Fridays and Saturdays, a floodlit Wurlitzer organ would majestically rise up from beneath the extensive, revolving stage before resident organist Bobby Pagan played the latest songs to the roar of a delighted audience.

The Hyams brothers and Major Gale invested an astonishing £250,000 in the building, quite a considerable sum, especially compared, for example, to the Odeon on Mile End Road which cost a mere £49,000. In September 1933, fourteen-year-old Bridget Hughes won the competition to officially open the Troxy on its first day. She was deemed to have been an extra special guest because she once lived on Caroline

Street which, as has been mentioned, ran alongside the cinema. Sadly but perhaps not surprisingly, the Troxy became part of the Gaumont circuit shortly after opening. Fortunately (and astutely) all of its directors joined the board at Gaumont soon after.

The stage was a facility that could revolve to offer four possible selections, with an orchestra pit that could be raised or allowed to remain hidden; such was its flexibility. Large numbers of stars and visiting orchestras would go on to appear at the theatre, including Ted Ray, Tommy Trinder, Will Hay and Louis Armstrong, among a plethora of others.

Its stage lighting incorporated a revolving colour screen batten created by one of its most popular managers, Maurice Cheepen. He periodically returned to manage the Troxy and was a man who knew how to put on a great show; perhaps the most bizarre aspect of his character being his penchant for animals. During a booking for a film entitled *Where no Vultures Fly*, a number of vultures, which were kept caged in the foyer area, made the local news after one of them escaped! There was even an occasion when a snake gave birth to six babies while on promotional duties at the theatre, and on another visit, a monkey developed such an affectionate bond with Mr Cheepen that only the manager could pick him up! He was an ingenious man who was awarded many showmanship stars from his employer in his time at the Troxy.

Exploring a local press photograph of a dour-looking Red Indian sitting astride a horse and handing out flyers which yelled 'The Indians are coming!' to advertise the Joseph Cotton picture *Two Flags West* (1950), you cannot help but laugh. Pantomimes were also regularly featured at the Troxy with *Cinderella* presented one Christmas, publicised by a horse and carriage trotting around the neighbouring streets carrying a giant pumpkin. In a period when animal welfare was not highly regarded, many visiting

The Troxy Cinema, Stepney, now Mecca Bingo.

circuses performed at cinemas across the country and in London, both the Troxy and the Avenue, in Ealing, were venues played at by such groups. Bengal tigers, captivity-bred lions and boxing kangaroos were all presented in what would have been quite a show.

During the Blitz, the East End was severely affected by German air raids, resulting in much of the district being flattened. The basement of the cinema was used as an air-raid shelter and one particularly heavy attack in September 1940 saw the Troxy narrowly escape being struck by a device that destroyed a neighbouring building. The Second World War had a profound effect upon the population there, so much so that by 1970, the population of the surrounding areas had fallen to two-thirds of what it was when the Troxy began its life in 1933.

If you were to search for the Troxy Cinema, alighting from Aldgate East underground and strolling down Commercial Road, in anticipation of seeing some of its picture past, unfortunately, there is not a great amount remaining to signal its celluloid playing days. Instead, it would be far better to visit the area beginning from the nearby Limehouse LDR station. The line runs directly behind the cinema and momentarily offers an unusual vantage spot, which, conveniently enough, has the Troxy within walking distance.

The cinema building still has a sprightly grandness and its beautifully commanding, yet understated veneer has an odd sense of refinement. Cream-coated faience tiling was favoured by its architect for the exterior, thanks to the adaptability, durability and ease with which it could be cleaned. A matching pair of flag-poles that once proudly displayed the Union Jack flag remain dormant but seemingly primed for a calling which is never likely to come.

It is a considerable structure in breadth and height, flowing along Pitsea and Caroline Streets before ultimately running back out onto Commerical Road. All the fire exits have been retained and the only element of the cinema design now appearing dated is the fact that there is scarcely any space for visitors to park their vehicles. While the Granada Cinema in Tooting actively saw private transportation as an integral part of their customer contingency, the Troxy was promoted within a 1930s environment whereby an emphasis was placed on the utilization of public transport.

There was definitely an air of quirkiness to life at the Troxy, with patrons somewhat eccentric in their behaviour. A good indication of this is in the cinema-goers consumption of shelled peanuts, once so popular with audiences that management had to request that visitors place their unwanted shells in the paper bags provided rather than discarding them on the auditorium floor. It was known that the man whose job it was to clean the building had great difficulty in picking up the shells with his vacuum cleaner and hence the request!

After lavish stage shows had been curtailed due to the 'call up' of many artistes and musicians, an emphasis was placed upon orchestra shows at the Troxy during the war years. By 1947, the joy of the pantomime had returned and the then Prime Minister, Clement Atlee, graced the theatre with his attendance during a matinee performance of *Cinderella*. There was nothing especially unusual about that, but what exactly made him arrive and depart by bus?

The most unusual element to the building was the cinema's main steel girder support for the balcony. It measured 110ft in length and was carefully transported down from the north of England, supported by a police escort, thus demonstrating the conviction upheld by the proprietors that nothing but the best could furnish their auditorium.

With its Magnescope screen enabling the more cinematic films of the day to be screened, the quintessential damsel-in-distress, Fay Wray, starred in the Troxy's first major feature: *King Kong* (1933). The initial programme offered the standard combination of cartoons and features mixed with a 'symphony of colour' showcase by resident organist Bobby Pagan. The show was rounded off with a second rendition of the national anthem and from then on, programmes changed weekly with a special Sunday show. Tickets generally cost 1*s* 6*d* and 2*s* for the circle area alongside 7*d* and 9*d* for the stalls. Both would be reduced for matinees and an in-house café/restaurant was open to the public and provided food at a very reasonable rate. By the mid-1990s, this part of the building, described by a Mecca bingo worker as 'maze like' remains closed.

The predominant feature of the vestibule was an impressive golden onyx staircase with multi-coloured marble flooring to dazzle visiting patrons. Once inside the building, the auditorium is a mightily impressive sight. A central, ornamental plaque dominates the ceiling, enhanced and perfectly complimented by the ornamental grille-work on the side wall, which worked in hiding the £15,000 air-conditioning system. The authentic three-coloured cove lighting found on both sides of the proscenium arch has been replaced by a Top Rank lighting system featuring an ugly digital display board. By November 1954, as the films got bigger, so did the apparatus to screen them. Cinemascope was installed with its first feature *The Black Shield of Falworh* (1954) starring Tony Curtis and Janet Leigh. Alas, this major development in film showmanship failed to save the cinema and in November 1960, it closed as a picture house. Rank, who had taken over the running of the place from Gaumont, found that dwindling audiences in such a vast hall, increasing costs and the arrival of television all played

Interior of the Troxy Cinema.

their roles with the East End set. *Siege of Sydney Street* (1960) was the final image to flicker across the screen at the Troxy on 19 November.

The start of the new decade was severe, not simply resulting in the closure of the Troxy Cinema but others, too. The Polar and Palaceium (opened in 1912) fell silent, all within a single East End mile. So what became of the building over the four decades since closure? In 1963 the Troxy reopened as a training school for blossoming opera singers and their coaching teams. Its exterior had hardly altered and the theatre was renamed the London Opera Centre. Its interior received a great deal of alteration work undertaken to adapt the property for its latest host. A lecture theatre was positioned in the rear stalls, with a total of 500 seats retained in the circle for intermittent operatic performances. It was the stage which incurred the brunt of the changes, being adapted to form an exact replica of Covent Garden Opera House. This consequently entailed extending the stage area over the top of the orchestra pit. Ironically, the architects responsible were George Coles & Co. Although its head designer died in the mid-1960s, his name and reputation lived on with his company trading until the early 1980s.

In the year when Robert De Niro won a best actor Oscar for his role in *Raging Bull* (1980), the development sub-committee of Tower Hamlets council deferred a final decision on a proposed plan to demolish the Troxy in favour of erecting a warehouse on its site. Meanwhile, the Troxy continued its decline after falling into disuse by the late 1970s. Fortunately, an intelligent solution was reached, whereby the building was granted a Grade II listing in 1981.

Just over ten years later found the Top Rank bingo club using the cinema for their latest bingo extravaganza, opening for business on 10 September 1992. A total of 1,958 seats were adapted and its crumbling glory was thankfully addressed with a £3 million modernisation policy realised with the guidance of English Heritage. The whole place was eventually repaired and repainted. A suspended ceiling was built into the foyer and the repainted walls coloured in lilac and pale blue, linking directly with the Mecca bingo signage exhibited on the front and side of the building.

Periodical photographs of the cinema confirm that the original Pitsea Street-facing advertising hoardings on the side of the theatre remain intact. Counterbalanced by four tiny, narrow windows, the space was given to promote new releases playing at the cinema during the coming weeks. Now though, it is blank and the Troxy name has since been replaced by the rainbow-coloured Mecca logo. It has been kept roughly in the same place as it always was, on the front façade. Another noticeable change, the precise date of its occurrence a mystery, concerns two, large mirrored fans clinging to either side of the same area. I do not believe the typical Art Deco shapes are authentic to the structure, as a September 1933 photograph of the same spot featured in the local *Star* newspaper shows no such adornments. Indeed, the space was used merely to advertise forthcoming attractions.

'There are no strangers at Stepney', invites the promotional leaflet issued by Rank at the end of the 1990s to advertise their bingo club, before concluding, 'Just friends you haven't met yet'. However, I will leave you with the Troxy pronouncement taken from the early 1930s, which is far more edifying: 'Where east meets west'.

9

Haringey & Wood Green

The areas of Hornsey, Tottenham and Wood Green joined together to form the London borough of Haringey in the mid-1960s and it is Turnpike Lane where we are headed, the general location for a host of former cinemas, including the Coronet, New Curzon, Coliseum and Gaumont Palace.

The Coronet Cinema

'An atmosphere of cheerful relaxation'

Implanted on the corner of Chingford Road and the Green Lanes junction, this cinema began flickering an image across its screen with its original name, the Ritz, on 30 December 1935. Here Clark Gable and Jean Harlow appeared together in *China Seas* (1935), which came to be the first picture supported by the anonymous, *Sing me a Song*. A cinema architecture publication of the period commented upon the arrival of the new venue and its associated shops: '[They] form a really notable architectural feature in a district peculiarly devoid of beauty'.

A point of attraction in its interior design consists in the use of coloured lighting and a large circular dome set in the middle of the ceiling of the 1,850 capacity auditorium. Its main staircase allowed visitors to reach the café lounge and the foyer to the large 600-seater balcony. An RCA sound system was brought in to round off an internal décor that the management hoped would 'produce an atmosphere of cheerful relaxation in which to enjoy the entertainment provided'. Ross Kinematograph projectors were installed so that patrons could, 'realise the benefits . . . that their eyes will show no sign of fatigue throughout the performance and no resultant eye strain'.

Apart from its corner-positioned entrance with a circular curvature and narrow metal window frames; such a delightful 1930s epitomization of a 'super cinema' establishment, there was not much to commend the peachy yellow Coronet. I use the past tense in describing the place because, during a sticky July 1999, after it had shut as a cinema on 23 March, the picture house and connecting (but independently run) restaurant and shops were bulldozed as part of a £4 million programme to rebuild and expand the bus station next to the cinema. Rumours hinting at the future use of the Coronet site for a purpose other than the cinema building go back to the mid-1980s, when the bus station regeneration plans were first outlined. The proposal was not

Right: The Coronet Cinema, Haringey.

Below: Side and rear view of the Coronet Cinema.

The Coronet Cinema shortly before demolition.

implemented earlier due to a lack of available investment. It was sad to observe the W.J. King-designed theatre being smashed to pieces, some sixty-four years after its opening. From the safety of the other side of the adjacent Duckett's Common, one can survey the New Curzon Cinema on Frobisher Road, now standing alone. It is ironic that when the obliteration of the capacious Coronet resulted in the tripling of the ABC-owned cinema in late September 1977, it was an act generally regarded as heralding the end of the single-screened Coronet. Loyal film-goers unusually began deserting their local for the improved selection of films now catered to at the improved Coronet of 625 seats in Screen 1, 417 seats in Screen 2 and 316 seats in Screen 3.

Patrons arriving there in the mid-1980s were confronted by a somewhat shabby and mostly darkened foyer and a worn auditorium. Still, while it was no palace, it was cheap and served the local populace well in providing an affordable social environment for north Londoners to patronize. I had the good fortune of visiting the creaky Coronet a couple of months before its closure and upon coming into the foyer, there was a small kiosk to the left and an additional pay desk on the right with circular-glazed doors taking the film enthusiast through another corridor towards all three screens. The large Screen 1 even had a decent sized screen.

The Coliseum Cinema

Forgetting the troubles of the day . . .

Along the busy roads of Haringey's Green Lanes and up towards where it meets with St Ann's Road was where the exact opening of a 'public amusements' centre remains unacknowledged. The Coliseum, a theatre with seating capacity for 641 people, began its life in 1910 as the Electric Coliseum Cinema and closed as a full-time picture house in June 1961. Although the building has partially remained in use since, its blue light-bulb façade signage has been neglected and abandoned. Apparently adapted as a warehouse in the 1980s, its presence as a former theatre is still substantial but, like the fellow Coliseum

The Coliseum Cinema, Haringey.

in Stoke Newington, this one had a gentility to its architecture reminiscent of a quiet, British Sunday afternoon: restrained yet absolutely dignified. In 1980, hidden behind a false stage façade, the original organ was discovered which was said to have last been played in the late 1920s. Covered in dirt, the two-manual organ was sold off when the building was gutted to make an extension for a furniture store.

Its paint and brickwork are crumbling, and the entrance and exit doors and the lettering of a round bingo sign have quickly faded, though the rear of the cinema building does have some function today. A sprawling furniture store, as mentioned, and a succession of varying retail outlets – a greengrocer and so forth, make good use of parts of the structure. A snooker club has also converged in a part of the interior of the old Coliseum theatre; with a camera-controlled entry point found along Green Lanes, or 'Salisbury Promenade' as it has been renamed in more recent times.

The Gaumont Palace

The cinema with a little touch of the unusual

While the often thunderous roar from innumerable car stereos and incessant traffic winds up and down the busy Broadway, onto the High Street and down towards Turnpike Lane, passers-by are diminished by the scale of the condensed frontage of the Gaumont Palace Cinema. Standing on a plot originally planned for a new atmospheric Astoria, its solid silver capital lettering was reinstated in 1993, when the building was the home of bingo, following the Grade II listing awarded to the old picture palace in 1990.

The established pale blue and peach coloured façade did not cloak the Gaumont until the arrival of the numbers game in September 1984; some eight months after the closure of the triple-screened cinema. Two additional High Road entrances, one of which led into a private club and is likely the original channel towards the former cinema café/restaurant, have both long since ceased trading and the main central cinema was coated in an curved aluminum jacket when I was living nearby. Long ago, its cinema café could easily have accommodated 170 patrons with the offer of coffee at 3*d* or other 'light refreshments at popular prices', enhanced by music played all day with free access for the public at large.

The cramped and constricted exterior belies the cool fluidity of its auditorium and I'm sure that architect William (W.E.) Trent, assisted by Ernest F. Tulley, was pleased at having another canvas upon which to rain forth his enchantments. If the nature of cinema construction in the 1930s was to involve swiftness of completion coupled with economy, then the Gaumont vaguely adhered. Building work was concluded in eleven months and with an audience capacity of a little more than 2,500 (2,600 or 2,556 have also been recorded), the scale of the project becomes clear. The depth of the cinema can be gauged by looking at the rear of the building from the supermarket behind and alongside it. Another decent view is from the central library, on The Broadway opposite the multiplex.

Opening day for the gleaming, modern Gaumont Palace was 26 March 1934, and by 1937, the Gaumont circuit became the sole owners of the theatre (having co-owned it with the APPH circuit previously). *The Constant Nymph* (1943) was rounded off with a stage performance by Bobby Howell and his band in a 'spectacular naval scene' followed by house-musician Frederic Bayco at the Compton organ. Tickets were priced at 9*d* in the front and rear stalls and 2*s* and 2*s* 6*d* for the front and rear circle.

Reflecting on its early days, I wonder what curious cinema-goers expected from this latest constellation? For a start, Trent, who worked on a number of Gaumont Cinemas all over Britain, adhered to the necessity of adapting to the space allocated for his cinema crafting. Instead of the more common painted, glazed earthenware (faience), he incorporated terrazzo facing over parts of the exterior brickwork. What this offered was the use of red and jade green colouring, which succeeded in complimenting the look. Trent, somewhat unusually, was unable to control all aspects of the interior design and plasterwork of this specific picture house; choosing a combination of apricot, blue and green converging upon red seats and carpeting. All this was rounded off with British walnut-garnered doors. Inside, the entrance halls were cloaked in marble mosaic designs and expensive, wooden walls were panelled almost up to the ceiling. Only then could patrons, having paid their admission charge, move to their seats along the ground floor or upstairs in the balcony; reached by a foyer with its ceiling covered in mirrors.

The Cinema Construction Journal of April 1934 spoke of the Gaumont as being 'a cinema with an unusual proscenium'. This defies a further unexpected feature found there: a semi-circular proscenium arch framing the 80ft x 30ft deep stage. The arch also had the regulatory steel-framed safety curtain and a beautiful design featuring the signs of the zodiac. From beneath the balcony, patrons in the 1930s could obtain a terrific perspective of the dreamily curved, streamlined architectural rhapsody. The fluidity of the walls meet the proscenium, and two narrow arches on either side of it emphasize its shape. Equally, the stage curtains also conformed to the mould of the arch. Stage wise, the Wood Green theatre was suitably furnished for visiting productions or film presentations, and included dressing rooms, an orchestra pit and a house organ,

The Gaumont Palace, Wood Green.

all playing different roles in a decent British picture house. Jack Hanbury was the first manager at the Gaumont and had gained valuable experience at the Broadway Cinema in Stratford and the Shepherd's Bush Pavilion, among other places.

On 9 September 1962, the Gaumont re-emerged as the Odeon. Yet, just over a decade later, at the end of December 1973, the biggest upheaval in the working life of the cinema building resulted in the introduction of three screens. Two mini-cinemas were positioned underneath the balcony; consisting of 149 and 150 seats, while the balcony and original screen continued as another cinema containing 814 seats, with 450 more located in the front stalls.

With its last reel set to roll, the Odeon Cinema, once the Gaumont, played on until 7 January 1984, with Disney's *The Jungle Book* and *Krull* being the final films on offer. Control of the then unlisted building fell into the hands of Top Rank which resulted in the removal of the mini-screens, with the auditorium used solely for bingo from 4 September 1984. This business carried on until its final 'house' was called in 1999. The building is now in use as a nightclub.

The Premier Electric Theatre

'The most unique picture theatre in London'. (1910 opening slogan)

The New Curzon Cinema, located off Green Lanes, started its commercial life as the Premier Electric Theatre on 16 April 1910, holding a total of 650 seats. It presented a combination of music hall variety acts and a sporadic moving picture treat; considered very much a novelty at the time, and all at 'popular prices'. Its architectural team consisted of William Emden and Stephen Egan, who devised the building for London Picture Theatre Ltd as part of their small chain of independent cinemas. Afternoon tea was served free of charge to new patrons during the Monday and Wednesday matinees and a 'brilliant programme of the world's premier animated pictures', a mix of comedy, sport, drama and travelogue, helped set the tone.

Audrey Field expounds in *Picture Palace: A Social History of the Cinema*, that, so long as the pictures on view moved, the actual subject matter was incidental. As the cinematograph developed, nobody in the fledgling business of public entertainment or cinematographic invention or presentation, let alone two of the pioneers of the latter, the Lumière brothers, believed that cinema would be the future. Hence, a full cinematographic licence was not obtained for the Electric until well into the 1950s (though, in any case, one was not legally required for variety houses to screen short filmic sequences). By 1932, the Turnpike Lane tube station opened, followed in 1935 by the modern ABC Cinema, unlocking its doors to the public literally next door to the underground.

Renamed the Vogue bingo club by November 1963, a year after the cinema was re-introduced as the Curzon in February 1964 and with a reduced seating totality of 500 available, it failed as such in less than three months. New seating and carpeting were coupled with a distinct family patronage. It would appear that the 1977 tripling of the neighbouring Coronet Cinema (*née* ABC in Turnpike Lane), proved to be the beginning of the end for the smaller venue here; even though the hugely cinematic 70mm film had been fitted. Just as many others were to discover that this specific type of film stock was expensive to produce as well as duplicate, and as soon as the product started to dwindle, the financial repercussions were acute. Adult films and Sunday Asian features played until 1989, when the Curzon closed due to lack of film product caused by the ABC venture. The Greater London Council (GLC) attempted to prohibit the adult films being shown, but as they had been awarded a certification by the BBFC, they continued.

The building was used as a laser game centre between 1990 and 1996, followed by occupancy by the Church of Destiny, an organisation which left soon after recognising the early stages of an intense deterioration common to such a building.

Ghostly goings-on took place in 1997 during the eleven months that it took to renovate the shell inherited by its new lease holder, a man named Jitu Ravall but known to everyone as 'JR'. During this time, two electricians, contracted to carry out a couple of days work at the Curzon. Rather than spend money on accommodation, the two men asked if they could sleep in the foyer area of the cinema, with the idea of using the cash saved to have a meal and a drink instead. JR agreed and offered them some blankets and pillows, suggesting that they bed down at the top of the small flight of steps immediately inside the street entrance.

The following day, one of the men asked JR if he had returned to the cinema on the previous evening, as he had felt someone step over him before making their way upstairs, open a nearby door and walk around inside. JR replied that he had. A second night passed and the exact same scenario was repeated. Upset by JR's apparent lack of trust in them (though in fact, there was nothing much of value in the building during the renovation works), one of the two men again broached the subject. This time, JR took the man to the door which he claimed to have seen opened during the two previous nights. It had been securely fastened as a security measure until the new leaseholder's commencement of work, and was therefore impossible to open. The electricians left their work unfinished and never returned.

Another time, a small, dedicated restoration team gathered together in the auditorium; cleaning, fixing and tending to various elements. One of the gang happened to look up towards the projection booth directly above and noticed a white beam of light pass across the port hole, giving the impression that somebody was in there. He made a point of mentioning this to the others and was informed that the electrical supply was suspect and not to concern himself. But it again showed itself, this time moving from the other side, and was again observed by the same young man. The explanation given to him was that the light therein was on a delayed timer switch which was why it appeared to come back on. Unbeknown to the young man, neither JR nor anyone else had been up to the box since renovation had began, as other tasks had demnaded attention first. Indeed, it proved to be quite a struggle to get into the box sometime later. The same young man who reported seeing the light anomaly also happened to be alone in the auditorium on another occassion when he was tapped on the shoulder, only to discover on turning that nobody was next to him. He too left the building somewhat swiftly.

The latest colourful Bollywood movies have been the predominant staple diet at the New Curzon since it opened as a 498-seater house in 1998. However, these, along with Greek movies, had been screened there from the late 1960s onwards when the building was known as the Curzon, written in huge capital letters above the entrance. There is more space now between the rows of seating and consequently, the screen at the New Curzon measures 32ft. (It was a little wider in the 1920s and was regarded as an above-average size for such a small theatre.) The screen has been moved in front of the original stage, with a flat ceiling being 6ft lower than the concave original. Unfortunately (or not), some two thirds of its authentic ceiling plasterwork was covered over to allow this. What has also changed is the frontage of the cinema; with one set of the three double-panelled entrance doors being blocked off. In addition, it can be observed, especially from looking at photographs taken in the 1920s, that much of the façade of the Regal, once the fourth largest chain in the country in 1941, has been transformed. The large, fin-like concrete block addition above the entrance now dominates the whole of its area. From an aesthetic and purely subjective viewpoint, I believe the alterations have been for the better.

The projection booth was not built into the theatre until the 1920s, and two dependable Kalee 20 projectors presented the moving images at the Curzon before being mysteriously removed and sold some time ago. One was seemingly purchased by the Duke of York's in Brighton (still open) and the other went to a Birmingham cinema. At present, projector 1 (its twin stands in the ABC Manchester) dates from the 1950s and number 2 from about 1922. A brass screen arch, dating from the 1920s, has been lost, though not, I might add, as a result of the latest renovations. There are two authentic details which can be found inside the entrance: a small brass handrail on either side of the foyer and, curiously, a small cast-iron safe, encrusted in concrete and positioned behind the ticket and sweets kiosk, located in roughly the same spot that it used to be. The keys to the safe were lost over thirty years ago, with only dynamite likely to open it now. Everything else related to the tradition of the cinema theatre was discarded many years since.

The Premier Electric Theatre, Haringey, later the New Curzon.

The New Curzon is the only Indian cinema in the north London area (at the time of writing), though competition springs forth from at least three others, including theatres in Edgware and Harrow. Its programming policy is to offer a nice mix of films; first and second-run features with four or more different titles on view every day. However, with the restrictive distribution policy of Asian films in the UK, there are four major distributors, each of whom make it a costly business for cinema's like the Curzon to screen films. That is, the major Indian blockbusters tend to play for a couple of weeks or so, with the right title obtaining a gross profit of £30,000 a week at times. In Haringey, audiences tend to shy away from violent titles, preferring the more family orientated Technicolour stories.

The existing team at the New Curzon are a friendly and dedicated bunch, and were fortunate in obtaining a managerial investment somewhere in the region of £250,000, required to bring the place up to date. The manager at the time would drive down from Birmingham every day to assist with the installation of a new auditorium ceiling and carpets, and helped with the floor and foyer repair work, replacing the lighting, sound system and seating. But with renewed competition from the Cineworld and Showcase multiplex venues in the High Street, the future of the New Curzon is in no way guaranteed.

The faded white veneer and extraordinary concrete curves of the Curzon come as a pleasurable surprise in the noisy confines of Turnpike Lane. The sultry, smooth form of this compact but hugely appealing little cinema, situated within an area once densely populated with picture houses, none of which have remained as functioning cinemas, makes the New Curzon a precious asset. This picture house has the honour of being the longest-running cinema (although not purpose-built) in the London area.

10

Southall

The Palace Cinema

'The most distinctive of all George Coles' cinemas . . . an astounding building'.
(David Atwel)

Completed in 1929, the year in which the Edward A. Stone Brixton Astoria Cinema astounded south London cinema-goers with its 'outside-in' enchantment, the Palace was the second Coles cinema to be revealed during the 1920s. His Commodore picture house in Hammersmith had opened in the early part of the year, prior to the late November inception of the Palace for United Pictures Theatres (UPT), a circuit which itself was soaked up by Gaumont-British in 1930.

The Palace provides a unique example of cinema architecture copying Chinese motifs, demonstrated by its coloured faience, tiled pagoda roof and four bold, gilded dragon heads. As Mr Coles clarified in the *Cinema Construction Journal* of 1930: 'The Palace Cinema was given a Chinese character thereby investing it with interest and stamping a new note not likely to be overlooked by the passer-by'. Settling upon the site of the old Paragon Palace Cinema, the place does not strike one as being so much out of place but out of time in its capacity as a working cinema. It is situated in an impoverished neighbourhood which I doubt has ever known anything else. Today, fly posters have swarmed over the exterior of the derelict theatre façade with promos for the latest Asian film releases, music magazines and concerts dominating the space. The Liberty shopping centre sign is still in place on the front of the South Street exterior, and it is a shame to see the decay and dirt ingrained in its haggard semblance.

The rooftop is where the building comes into its own; festooned with the heads of four dragons coated in golden skin, their tails and elongated bodies giving life and fluidity of movement to the architecture, as if the creatures are guarding the place. It looks as if all of its slight external structural detailing remains under a heavy coating of pollution and fumes from the dirty, busy street. The plasterwork around the main entrance has suffered the most in the intervening years, but it would not take too drastic an amount of renovation to recapture its glorious roar. In 1980, the Palace was listed as a building of outstanding architectural merit, a reference directed predominantly at its exterior, beyond which its façade is a plain brick construction. The rear of the Palace building was at some point the home of the *India Times* publishing and printing company as well as a hair salon. The rear of the structure also has a Liberty Market Hall sign from the mid-1980s, accompanied by scattered strips of concrete on the ground and signs informing of the 'demolition in progress'. The whole area is in fact closed off and securely locked up.

In 1950, the 1,740-seater Palace Cinema became the Gaumont until Odeon took on the challenge in 1961; concluding its ownership in June 1971. The preceding year saw the cinema reopen as the Godeon in January, followed by yet another change in name with the Liberty, a distributor of Indian films, re-labelling the picture house as the Liberty Cinema. The last films to be screened were in 1982, from which point the theatre transformed into an indoor market and shopping centre.

Above: The Palace Cinema, Southall.

Left: Rooftop dragon motifs of the Palace Cinema.

11

Notting Hill & Bayswater

The Electric Cinema

'London's friendliest cinema'

The Notting Hill Electric Cinema Theatre was the first in a pack of cinemas operated by Harry Hymason. His stipulation that any further use of this specific building could only be in the form of a cinema acted as a double-edged sword, maintaining its survival but starving it financially. Construction started at 191 Portobello Road on the 600-seater picture palace in 1910, on space formerly occupied by a timber yard. With its ornate wall and roof frieze, barrel-vaulted roof and specifically enclosed projection booth (as films at that time consisted of highly flammable nitrate stock), the Edwardian Baroque splendour of the Electric was to set a precedent for cinema design. This was in spite of the fact that it was to fall in the ferociously developing cinema industry of the early 1990s. The building was created by Gerald Seymour Valentin, and being erected in the days when the pictures were silent and noise was directed *at* the screen from its vociferous audience below; there was no requirement for acoustic consideration in his design. Cinema-goers were invited in to the Electric on 27 February 1911, through a ticket price of 3*d* or 6*d*. A reserved seat was available which cost a little more than a shilling, with the added incentive of a free orange and a bun!

From Notting Hill Gate tube station, where the Gate and Coronet Cinemas manifest themselves, we head down the hill towards Portobello Road, where a collection of antique shops and pubs welcome the pilgrim in search of the Electric Cinema. Being in the area anytime in the summer of 1999, one could observe a mass of Far Eastern tourists excitedly taking turns to be snapped outside the bookshop where Hugh Grant's character in *Notting Hill* initially meets and falls for Julia Roberts (or was it the other way round?) In the film, there is a brief, heavily fly-posted exterior shot of the lower façade of the Electric Cinema, a smaller than imagined hall with a fluid and inviting exterior.

It has been documented that during the First World War, the Electric was attacked by a mob after its manager, a German, was rumoured to be signalling to Zeppelins from the top of the building. Another manager was said to be running a glue factory at the same time as being employed at the cinema, and, for a jar of cod heads, he would allow patrons inside in lieu of purchasing a ticket. It has also been rumoured that mass murderer John Chrisite was at one time a projectionist at the cinema. David Putnam, the film producer, viewed the Imperial as 'the temple of cinema' and throughout its

The Electric Cinema, Notting Hill.

working life, it was a picture palace that generated genuine affection among staff, patrons and the media alike. *Time Out* labelled it 'London's friendliest cinema', while eminent *Guardian* film critic Derek Malcolm added, 'The Electric has done more to widen the cinematic horizons in London . . . than practically any other cinema'.

In the 1960s, when 501 million people visited cinemas across the country (falling to 193 million by the end of the decade), the Imperial remained little changed from its past days, its small and confined foyer and endearingly shaped pay box had been left pretty much as they had always been. The mosaic floor tiling of the Electric was maintained, but its reputation was underpinned as a typically bad example of the lowliest-kind of bug house, with an auditorium falling apart around an ageing audience, un-flummoxed by the prospect of entire rows of seating collapsing, should anyone be unwise enough to sit in them. On particularly wet days, entire areas were cordoned off due to the effect of flooding. Yet still, the Imperial soldiered on, with no investment made in its infrastructure. It was in the late 1960s when the Electric Cinema Club was given access to present a late-night Saturday show that the tide began to turn for the cinema. Fridays and Saturdays now catered to an audience interested in the latest features, as well as seeing older films, and alternative and more unusual films that struggled to find a venue in London. Luis Brunel's *Criminal Life of Archiboldo de la Cruz* (1955) was the first feature. The cinema club had been making more money on its two or three evenings than the poorly-attended Imperial could manage all week and it proved to be such a triumph that in 1970, the Imperial closed and the Electric Cinema Club took on the running of the building full-time.

Financial investment at last came in December 1970, when it was agreed that £50,000 would be spent on fresh seating and sound and projection equipment, among other things. Two 35mm projectors were brought in after being salvaged from the private screening room of the late Sir Winston Churchill. Fortuitously, the proscenium arch at the Electric had not been altered, even after the arrival of differing screen ratios for Cinemascope, due to the management not wanting to spend any money, so it was simply masked off to enable such features to be presented. Further financial gusto was needed to make the additional repairs to the structure of the decrepit building but, although promised by the overall owners (not the ECC), they were not carried out in full. By 1968, the Imperial had reached its lowest ebb with no heating available in the auditorium. It had been rushing downhill since the late 1950s, when competition from the arrival of the nearby Odeon Cinema in Westbourne Grove, cast a shadow. The Imperial's survival was demonstrated by its cheap admission charge and its convenience for inebriated patrons, fresh out of the pubs, to sleep away afternoons while an indefinite flow of George Raft gangster pictures and Audie Murphy Westerns vacuously shone across the screen. Audiences consisted not only of locals but of people who had travelled across London to dwell in the adventurous delights of *Flash Gordon* serials and Einstein epics. Times were changing.

The Electric Cinema Club commemorated its tenth birthday in 1980 and marked its celebrations by further refurbishment consisting of new seating, central heating and additional aspects applied with a management sensitivity, which, according to the celebratory booklet, aimed at 'not becoming as antiseptic and dull as most cinemas these days'. Late-night shows continued with sci-fi, horror and supernatural themes, including *Quatermass and the Pit* (1967) and *Westworld* (1973). Commendably, the film club was somehow able to survive without the cushion of any grants or arts/public bodies by providing a level of diversity which singled it out, along with the National Film Theatre, as unique among other London cinemas. 'Their policy,' began *Time Out*, 'is simply to put on anything that's good of its kind'.

Over a considerable period, the Electric held the record of being the oldest purpose-built picture house in operation in Britain due to there being no documented record of it ever having closed. Alas, the cinema shut its doors on 31 October 1983 and was purchased by Mainline Pictures. Theatre staff wanted to take over the running of the cinema but their bid ultimately failed and the Electric Screen became its latest title. Its prospects of longevity were destroyed by the new management's insistence on changing the programme schedule, which had made it its name, in favour of a single, latest release picture being shown. During the course of surface renovations, new seats and Dolby stereo sound were introduced, while segments of plasterwork were revealed in the auditorium. But structural repairs which would have cost more to address were neglected.

In April 1987 the cinema was sold, with no plans to open it once more as a cinema being voiced by its latest proprietors, Central Properties. A shockwave quickly followed through patrons and staff alike and a campaign to 'Save the Electric' was founded

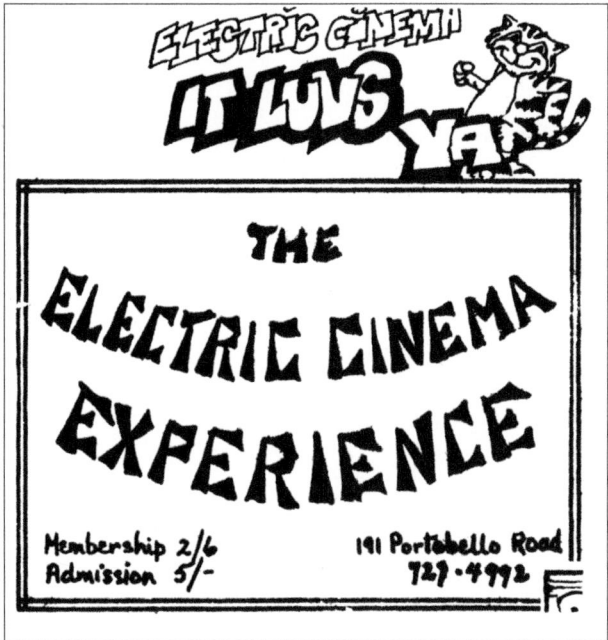

(a petition was eventually signed by 10,000 people, including Anthony Hopkins and Julie Christie). Mainline and Central kept comments to the media to an absolute minimum and the immediate fate of the building appeared to be rushing forth. The cinema closed for good on 6 May 1987 and its final curtain fell with a distinctly bitter taste after the owners brought its closure forward a day. This was a familiar ploy engaged by many cinema proprietors at failing picture houses in the 1970s and '80s to minimise any public outcry. Scant regard was shown towards members of staff, the majority of whom were unaware of the new plans and dutifully went along to collect their pay on the day following closure, only to find the locks on the building changed and all access denied.

The Electric would re-remerge as the Imperial Theatre by 1991; in a period when a choice of three varying double bills helped sustain its local clientele within the confines of a pretty, Classically decorated interior. Miraculously, July 2000 saw *Time Out* confirm the sale of the building to Peter Simon, founder of the Monsoon stores. Today the cinema is once again open for business.

The Coronet Cinema

'All the latest triumphs of the picture world thrown onto the Coronet screen'.
(1930s cinema slogan)

In a poignant moment from *Notting Hill,* a dour and bespectacled Hugh Grant sits up in the dress circle at the Coronet – a scene which is noteworthy in that it provides a revealing view of the cinema auditorium. The Coronet also featured as a location in the 1989 film adaptation of the Martin Amis novel, *The Rachel Papers,* with it doubling-up in a dubious cameo performance as an adult cinema.

The Coronet Cinema, Notting Hill.

It was as a theatre that the Coronet came into fruition back in November 1896; with W.G.R. Sprague, a theatre architect of some repute, devising a 1,143-seater venue with a twist. Sprague was an industrious designer and his surviving West End theatres have all been listed as being of architectural interest. His past glories include the Camden Palace (now a nightclub), and the Wyndhams, Aldwick, Globe, Lyric, Queen's and Albery Theatres. However, in an ironic twist of fate, the Coronet, 'A small opera house with an orchestra pit big enough to stage Wagner' (*The Independent*, 1989) was the only entry in the above set failing to secure a statutory listing. Remarkably, it would only receive a Grade II protective level in 1989, when a threat of structural redevelopment knocked at its door.

As a theatrical venue, with a 65ft x 40ft stage, dressing rooms and orchestra pit 'luxuriously decorated in the Louis XVI style', the Coronet enjoyed the patronage of many thespians, including Sarah Bernhardt in *La dame aux Camelias*, along with visitations from leading Italian operatic companies, as well as premièring a large number of other operas such as *La Boheme* and *Zaza*. The theatre could lay claim to being the first to present an English language performance of both Wagner's *Siegfield* and *The Magic Flute*. From 1921, the seating capacity was reduced to 1,100 and eventually receded to 919 in 1943 and 569 by 1961. The reason for this was primarily owing to the introduction of films on a permanent basis in 1916. Theatrical shows ran concurrently, but as a theatre, the Coronet was not a consistent success and, consequently, the original theatre boxes were removed and the gallery area fell into disuse by 1923, all of which explained the reduction in seats.

That same year was the final period in which theatrical shows were offered by the Coronet (though a contradicting source gives 1940 as its concluding year). Whichever year is correct, with the arrival of the Second World War, the Coronet was open throughout the conflict and would appear to have been unaffected by the hostilities. Its interior has remained almost intact since an 1898 publication called *The Era* commented after visiting, 'The scheme of decoration is a harmony of cream, chrome and gold, and a striking feature is the handsome floriated columns that rise each side of the boxes near the proscenium, of which there are eight . . . their construction being novel and picturesque'.

After the war, the Coronet Cinema flew under the Gaumont circuit flag and, from 1950, became the Gaumont Cinema. Gaumont-British had briefly controlled the building in 1937, in among a further half a dozen or so other lease holders, including the PCT circuit in 1939, and with another change in 1949.

The Rank Organisation was the first company which attempted to utilise the large theatre in plans that no longer included its use as a working cinema. Their 1973 redevelopment scheme, which was rejected by the Royal Borough of Kensington & Chelsea, would have seen the theatre's re-emergence as a shopping centre and office complex. What this showed was the fact that the Coronet was extremely vulnerable to development by investors due to its non-listed status. A 1979 application to the Department of the Environment had failed and its life was left hanging in the balance.

McDonalds had been unsuccessful in their quest to buy the nearby Gate Cinema in 1987 and had returned a couple of years later with the Coronet set to become their 307th fast-food outlet. As soon as these plans became known publicly, a campaign to save the Coronet Cinema began, consisting predominantly of local residents but also involving the Theatre Trust and, to a lesser extent, English Heritage. 'The preservation of the Coronet', emphasized campaign leader Stella Wright in a local newspaper in 1989, 'is not just a local issue. It should concern the whole of London and world-wide audiences to stop profit-making concerns ruining yet another part of our history and environment, with there being a dozen other restaurants within yards of the Coronet including a Wimpy.'

Not everyone was as concerned with sustaining a local landmark. Some interests were closer to home: 'We simply do not want a garish coloured McDonalds here', bemoaned a local member of Campden Hill Residents' Association, 'or their uniformed staff'. Public disquiet had seemed to sway the decision that rescued the Gate Cinema from earlier redevelopment – but could the same be said for the life of the mighty Coronet? The reasonable middle ground in the debate was articulated by Councillor Rima Horton, a member of the K&C Town Planning Committee; 'Junk food is more profitable than cinema or theatre', conceded the local member in a May 1989 in a letter to the *Guardian*. 'In a sane world, attention would be paid to both commercial profit and community use. Beauty would have a value even if it didn't appear on the balance sheet.' Of course, what Councillor Horton said here was echoed by the planning committee itself; which had to address McDonald's proposal objectively or on aesthetic grounds, could not eliminate such a working procedure adopted by the Borough Council.

The Coronet Cinema, showing the neighbouring Gate Cinema.

Andrew Lloyd Webber's Really Useful Company and a host of other groups all showed a seeming interest in making use of the Coronet as a theatre which, unlike the Electric Cinema on Portobello Road, could be found conveniently on the High Street, with a tube station within sight of the building. Playwright Christopher Hampton, who had an office which looked out at the cinema in the distance, placed the issue in context: 'It could be an ideal local theatre', he offered in the *Sunday Times* (July 1989). 'There's a shortage of 400–5,550-seaters, a nice size, ideal these days'.

Concern also grew with the imminent opening of the new Whiteley's multiplex cinema in the nearby area of Bayswater but, as time has shown, both the Coronet and the new complex (and not forgetting the Gate Cinema) have all managed to survive. In the midst of all this uncertainty, two local businessmen attempted to purchase the remaining lease of the Coronet from its lease-holder, Panton Film Distributors (the same company involved with the Electric Cinema), with a proposal to turn the building in to a cabaret theatre and associated restaurant. Speaking in the *Kensington News*, one of the duo began: 'We say give the theatre back to the area and let's make it a linchpin of social intercourse'. And so, more than a decade later, the Coronet Cinema remains open, in need of renovation in one of its two screens but having seen many alternate plans fall by the wayside.

The Gate Cinema

The voice of little brother

Trading under the Oasis Cinema banner since the 1970s, the exterior of the Gate Cinema on Notting Hill Gate is almost nondescript in comparison to the obvious immensity of the fellow Coronet Cinema. Both have made their homes on the same stretch of west London space, only a few doors from each other. The Gate is one of a trio of picture houses that make up a circuit which includes the Ritzy in Brixton and the Cameo in Edinburgh. Its diminutive external demeanor is one of a scaled down homage to Mies van der Roehe; all straight lines embellished with no obvious ostentation and succeeding in being purely functional. The non-listed Gate evokes an office block feel to its architecture and the place seems little changed since its instigation in the early 1940s as the 307-seater Embassy News Theatre. The Embassy, as it was known by 1946, was one of the few theatres at the time solely in use as a newsreel venue rather than as a more traditional feature film house. However, this novel existence was curtailed in 1957 with the genesis of the Classic Repertory Cinema, known as the Classic until 1974 when the current name was introduced.

In the period of time when the cinema was called the Classic, a savoury concession, tempting passing residents and film-goers with its selection of home-made chocolates and patisseries, once used the area that is now a cash desk. As one comes into the auditorium, the long confined hall seems to come from an entirely separate era than its exterior visage. It is a comfortable space to find oneself in, with an understated yet pleasing décor giving off a music hall sensation even though no stage is found here. What it has in abundance is an ambience completely and curiously at odds with the starkness of its façade, including adjoining lavatories entered to the right of the screen, which add to the overall quaintness of the Gate Cinema.

Presently, the Gate has a programming policy offering the option for local film makers to have their short features shown to an audience prior to the main film, a concoction of European art house and world cinema productions. After a brief closure in 1984, the cinema reopened the following year and has been happily making a decent living in a business area with its big brother, the Coronet Cinema, and the multiplex in Bayswater.

Queens Cinema

Fluid and evocative curves . . .

Sitting at 98 Bishops Bridge Road at the point where it meets Queensway, in the cosmopolitan centre of W2, is the beige-fashioned Queens, now wearing the shiny badge of an American-themed restaurant since 1995. Being just one among a group of more than thirty eateries, the old cinema offers a dual outward impression to the passer-by, wholly dependent upon whether it is seen during the day or at night. Its fluid and evocative curves are suggestive of Art Nouveau and the manner of the building appeals to the eye at whatever time of visiting.

Suburban cinemas such as this often presented brightly toned exotica by way of an external glazed tiled appearance, inspired by contemporary American designs popular at the time. At the cinema there is a mosaic-tiled 'Queens' title in red lettering made up of a storm of a blue, green and orange Aztec pattern scheme far above what was the original entrance. Its pretty window configuration beneath this is the defining feature of the cinema, with three strips of characteristically 1930s narrow windows on either side of an additional trio, which produces a melodic sensation to this pleasing J. Stanley Beard & Clare design.

The Classic Cinema, which later became the Gate Cinema, 1960s.

The natural light enhancements of orange, green and aqua are lit up each evening, but regrettably, the centralised main entry point which guided patrons into the theatre for some sixty years is no longer used. In fact, without having seen a photograph of the building in its cinema heyday, it would not be immediately apparent that it was ever there, due to a row of windows running along its space presently disguising the location of a significant feature of the redundant Queens Cinema. Unusual for its day, a vertical Queens sign was to be found to the left of the main façade (incorporated onto its brickwork) which has since been lost and effectively replaced by a duet of TGI Friday's branding, clearly defining the intent of the present business. Immediately beneath this was a corner shop called the Kiosk; possibly sub-let by the cinema proprietors and itself now providing an entrance/exit facility adopted as one of two used by the restaurant. The restaurant chain purchased the listed structure in 1994 and restrictions, or rather protective implications, manifested themselves when the company was denied planning permission for brass menu boards to be erected outside the building. Additional aspects of the listing also mean that the colour scheme at the Queens cannot be altered (something ignored by the present owners of the Gaumont in Wood Green).

Opened on 3 October 1932, the 1,428-seater Queens Cinema would see the arrival of new management by February 1935 and again in 1962 with the ABC chain. Tripling came in September 1975 with a 436-seater Screen 1, 224-seater Screen 2 and 213-seater screen 3, pre-dating the eight-screen UCI complex in the nearby Whiteleys shopping centre by some fourteen years. The latter multiplex opened in December 1990 with the features, *Ghostbusters II* and *Shirley Valentine*. Meanwhile, the eventual demise of the Queens came in 1988.

The Queens Cinema, Notting Hill.

The mosaic tiled lettering and 1930s style windows of the Queens Cinema, now TGI Friday's.

12

Swiss Cottage

Odeon Swiss Cottage

'Just around the corner at the O-deon' (1930s promotional song)

A faded shadow of antiquated Odeon lettering lingers as a reminder to the past, high above the shiny new branding of condensed silver and blue, quintessentially positioned on the canopy running along the length of this 1937 brown-bricked frontage. As such, its location now marks a row of several narrow panelled windows originally positioned as a centre point to the balance of the building. A massive structure, the Odeon sits next to the quaintly-titled Ye Olde Swiss Cottage public house; a property dwarfed by the curving, twirling and interweaving nature of the theatre exterior.

The vision for Swiss Cottage was carried through from Odeon's Birmingham based architectural office which was headed by Harry Weedon. It was the first house to be planned by him but in actuality, the 2,115-seater Odeon was designed by Basil Herring, from the plans of Robert Cromie. Clearly, its shape is not felt to be typical of the circuit and instead it has been acknowledged as being more akin with Cromie's work for the Regal circuit of cinemas, such as those found in Hammersmith, Kingston-upon-Thames or Wimbledon. As architectural controller for the entire Odeon chain, Weedon was entrusted to fulfill the desire that Oscar Deusch had for making every Odeon recognisable throughout the country by way of a visual impact. This was to show itself in the form of a trademark vertical tower on its exterior. Above all else, Deusch sought a unified functionality to all his theatres, in particular, the ones constructed from his West Midlands HQ. 'So not only was he building cinemas with other people's money', added architect Robert Bullivant who worked for Odeon in 1935, 'but he was furnishing it and equipping it at comparatively little cost. And this was one of the reasons for the success of his ventures'.

Deusch personally attended the opening charity gala for his latest Odeon (the 220th) on 4 September 1937 and along with Weedon, a horde of prestigious names were also in attendance. Film director Alexander Korda and popular actors of the period, Merle Oberon and Conrad Veidt, joined guests after the show in dancing on the stage well into the early hours. 'The romance of Odeon that is perfect in entertainment', a 1930s newsreel proclaimed.

Returning spirits from the past would be confronted with great confusion if venturing back into the cinema building nowadays; six mini-screens compete in a modified

The Odeon, Swiss Cottage.

interior with scarcely a glance at the heritage of years gone by. Actors would have been confronted with gigantic mosaic mirrors combined in space, which were regarded as exceptional in terms of design. The circle was reached by either of two staircases in the lobby, which then flowed into a second, at which the balcony could be entered through an additional point of access. Glancing down from above, cinema-goers could see an array of fine grille work and artificial pillars coated in green, blue and gold jackets. A glimpse of the in-house Compton Theatre organ (removed in 1964), with its illuminated console, added to a jolly combination of treats for film fans.

The 1960s saw musical presentations and a number of Sunday night concerts, but the removal of the Compton was to be the beginning of the end for such events at Swiss Cottage and by 1973, the Odeon was recorded as the thirteenth of the Rank-owned chain to be converted into a three-screen multiplex. Some 780 patrons could now be welcomed into Screen 1, 109 in the gold-painted Screen 2 and 105 in the turquoise realms of screen 3. *The Ragman's Daughter, Fiddler on the Roof* and *Hammersmith is Out* came together to initiate proceedings on 25 February 1973. Consequently, and without a doubt, such a radical project had a devastating effect on the former 1,282-seater auditorium. The repercussions were manifest, with half of the original seating being lost in the course of the £35,000 reconstruction. Cinema fans were now offered a broader choice of films (whereby the circuit could attract more patrons by increasing their volume of consumable product) and were charged an admission fee of 40p, 45p and 50p for Screen 1 and 60p for either of the two other screens.

The clichéd but somehow apt phrase 'only in the movies' could be applied to what happened next at the Odeon: in 1986, Rank almost agreed to a scheme that would have seen the demolition of their cinema in favour of building a smaller one. This would have been with the added incentive of lucratively-priced apartments being part of the new complex. Tragically, Rank was to freely voice the fact that they ruined the balance of the authentic single-screen auditorium through their own 1973 tripling and, subsequently, the cinema/housing plan failed to come to fruition. A few years ago, after the Swiss Cottage Odeon had resiliently marched on, the building had its screen capacity doubled to six in a scheme costing £600,000. And still, regardless of the relatively recent arrival of the 8-screen Vue O2 multiplex (initially the Warner Village), also on Finchley Road, and within walking distance of the Odeon, the boldness of this old-timer is to be applauded.

13

Brixton

At the southern most tip of the Victoria tube line is Brixton, a district whose reputation precedes it. And as is the case with such notoriety, our visit is validated by our exploration of four theatres, albeit only one of which, the Ritzy, remains as a working cinema. Nonetheless, all are worth the energy to seek out. Between 1910 and 1915, there had been at least nine cinemas in one form or another in operation here, and the shells of Pyke's Cinematograph Hall, the Astoria and Palladium can still be visited, as can the ghost of an anonymous hall last in use as a London Electric office along Brixton Road.

Brixton Astoria Cinema

'Lit by a crescent moon and stars which twinkled . . . ' (1929 advertisement)

Springing forth from the conveniently-located underground station, one first takes a right turning, and within five minutes or so, the semi-domed marvel of the Astoria Cinema comes into view. Just up from the main road, Stockwell Road is dominated by this 2,892-seater picture house currently prospering as a live music venue, Brixton Academy. The hall was the first of four Astoria venues built for a company with substantial financial backing from Paramount Pictures, their others being in Streatham (later an Odeon), Old Kent Road and Finsbury Park. Costing £250,000 to construct and furnish, the Brixton Astoria had a proposed seating capacity of 4,500, a figure capped for safety reasons, and it opened in its revised form on 19 August 1929 with the Al Jolson talkie *The Singing Fool* (1929).

Edward Stone was appointed chairman of the new company formed to take on the running of the Astoria chain and is wrongly cited as being the designer of the building when, in fact, the team of T.R. 'Tommy' Somerford & Ewen Barr devised the blueprint. Built upon the land once in use as a private garden, its inauguration was a great success with the public, demonstrated by a queue for tickets which started that midsummer morning. With its semi-domed exterior entrance made up of copper within a background of cream and green faience, generous rehabilitation work was undertaken in 1999, repairing the crumbling stonework of this smaller-than-imagined façade and carried out by the Heritage Lottery Fund.

Investigating its demeanour during the onset of a recent winter, the side of the Astoria as it is seen along Stockwell Road, is in fine condition. Its steel window frames painted a rugged red, the general scale of the cinema becomes clear after walking behind the rear and returning via the same road. Its hugeness is made evident upon strolling down Astoria Walk, which returns the visitor to the main entrance.

The original 'VARIETY', 'CINEMA' and 'ASTORIA' capital lettering (positioned on the left, right and horizontally centred respectively) have been repaired in more recent years. Interestingly, when the theatre was home to the Odeon, their five letters were also placed on the frontage but above the Astoria titling. Its external appearance, entrance aside, is not especially appealing; with an odd exposure of brick showing along Astoria Walk, providing a purely functional look. Shops accommodating a travel agency, bookmakers and locksmiths complete its Stockwell Road front.

Possibly in keeping with the wonders of the Finsbury Park Astoria (sure to be a favourite as soon as your eyes cast upon it), the Brixton Astoria also includes a foyer-situated fountain complete with fish. A stage spanning 100ft x 40ft in its cinema days was set off by a proscenium arch that once had mechanical figures moving across it to supplement the sense of depth. Vast illustrative detailing on its auditorium walls generated a three-dimensional perspective enhanced by a fusion of columns, false balconies and balustrades topped off with a mass of foliage that was often mistaken for real but consisted of elaborate plasterwork. A domed, 18,000 sq-ft ceiling would have a night sky scene specially projected over it, while on stage, the sound emanating from the Compton organ completed the rapture for the senses.

Rank shut the established Odeon Astoria as a cinema in 1972 with the lackadaisical Charles Bronson flick *Red Sun* (1971) on 29 July. Lumbered with a theatre too vast for a dwindling cinema clientele and, equally, too expensive to both heat and maintain, voices

The Brixton Astoria Cinema, now the Brixton Academy.

The old Brixton Astoria Cinema is currently a popular live music venue.

at Rank felt that the final reel in the life story of the Brixton Astoria had been well and truly played. Yet following these final days, when only the circle had been open, the Sundown, a music and disco club, was to breathe new life into the old place, beginning in September of that year. However, by the following January, Rank had once more been forced to close its doors when the latest venture proving to be a flop. Another proposal to turn the building into a skateboarding rink was eventually discarded, resulting in its present, let alone future, looking decidedly bleak. The usual prospect of demolition and other non-viable schemes were trotted out while the theatre languished as a company warehouse. Thankfully, a Grade II and subsequent Grade II* listing preserved the life of the Astoria indefinitely.

More than a decade later, 12 March 1982 to be exact, the Fair Deal concert hall revived the old picture house as the latest live music haunt. A gig by Birmingham's finest, UB40, opened proceedings. In the process of this change, the building was restored at a great financial expenditure, which clearly played its role in the early demise of the business later that same year. Incredibly, in what was now becoming known as the Academy, the Astoria opened again on 7 October 1983 as the Brixton Academy. Its shell was not in great condition, but it has since been consistent in upholding the dictum of what the place has always been about: entertainment.

The Rolling Stones, Bruce Springsteen, Bob Dylan, The Clash and Wham have all played at the hall, which can accommodate 4,000 people – 3,500 in the stalls and the remainder in the balcony. One music fan ended up in hospital after jumping from the balcony during a manic show for the American punk band, The Offspring. The building has, in more recent years, been owned by the McKenzie Group which was provided with a grant to improve the old cinema both inside and out. A commemorative double CD album called *Academy – Celebrate the True Anthems* was released in May 2000, which is worth collecting if only for its night-time exterior photograph of the building.

The Ritzy Cinema

'What you need is something a little bit ritzy . . . '

As one returns onto the Brixton Road, and again pass the tube station (but in the opposite direction), Brighton Terrace on the right-hand side was where the Granada Cinema (formerly the Empress Variety Theatre) bowed out as a bingo club prior to demolition in November 1992. On the side of the building which saw Max Miller having audiences roll in the aisles, a housing complex now stands.

On a more optimistic note, our second picture house in nearby Brixton Oval is a perennial favourite: the Ritzy. Situated adjacent to the library and opposite Lambeth Town Hall, the Ritzy established itself as the Electric Pavilion on 24 March 1911. It was only the second cinema in the capital specifically built to be a movie house. A succession of angelic cherubs holding shields with the initials 'EP' emblazoned upon them can be seen above the diminutive entrance which, while in pristine condition, seems reminiscent of the stern of a ship. Over the years, which were often harsh to the building, all of this rich detailing was hidden from public view in favour of disastrous work done in the 1970s which rendered its appearance unrecognisable from that of today's finery. Following on from the life of the Electric Pavilion, the 850-seater Pavilion Cinema became the Pullman on 31 August 1954, preceding the arrival of the Classic Cinema in May 1964.

As the Classic, the cinema lasted just over two years, coming to an end on 5 June 1978, at which point the proprietor removed every seat before abandoning the building. A further eighteen months of dereliction damaged the infrastructure of the theatre and resulted in damage to its roof as well as general vandalism. It was in 1978 that the most important chapter in the life of this little cinema became a real 'page-turner', with the arrival of a group of five business partners including a housewife, a civil servant and a student, the outcome of which set the foundations for the future of the Ritzy which are still firmly set today.

The fusion of such an assortment of personnel sprang forth after one of them read about the demise of the building in a local newspaper and decided to act. And a later advertisement in the listings magazine *Time Out* found investors each contributing £10,000 to take on the running of the place. Six months later, with a month which included solely clearing the junk and debris in the auditorium before any rendering or in-depth cleaning could be enabled, evening performances (with late shows too) costing £1 in admission, set the wheels in motion. Despite the roof still leaking, a mixture of double bills played at the theatre for a week or so. Carpeting was replaced and 491 seats, all having to be adapted, were purchased from the fallen Studio 1 Cinema on Oxford Street/Tottenham Court Road. A friend of Theo Sheppard's, one of the group's partners, came up with the eventual name of the cinema: 'What you need is something a little bit ritzy . . .'

Programming was to consist of films which would not necessarily find a sufficient outlet at other cinemas, aspiring to first run presentations. The latest Woody Allen comedy, *Manhattan* (1979) showed that the Ritzy could hold its own when it was given a first-run simultaneously with the West End houses. Live concerts followed in September and in a couple of years, a set of seven staff members were employed to meet the needs of close to 15,000 film-goers each week at the only independent cinema in south London. Its reputation at this time was one with a left wing slant, showing a combination of art house and gay interest pictures. Consistent with their ethos, the management was keen to involve local groups in utilising the Ritzy as a community resource. Lambeth Council gave the proprietors an eighteen month rent-free respite with the stipulation that all renovation needs had to be executed by the group. Externally, the place was a mess: a dour squared façade with no sign of the original architectural accoutrements visible, and combining pink and green with yellow and green, depending upon which part of the structure you happened to be looking up at.

The Ritzy Cinema, Brixton.

Lambeth Council bought the cinema in the early 1980s and had already canvassed opinions as to how the tired old building could be maximised. (A carpet warehouse and demolition were two options seriously considered.) Following on from the Brixton riots of 1981, and not aided by a weak art house selection of films, the Ritzy almost went under. An idea to adapt the library annexe next to the cinema into a bar was successfull, and it is still open today. By 1985, a staff of fourteen made certain that the picture house ran smoothly and following 1986, a total of 15,000 members each contributed an annual membership of 30p to the upgraded Ritzy Cinema Club. On average, a dozen films were exhibited each week.

The five-screen Ritzy Cinema (with 352, 179, 118, 108 and 184 seats in each screen respectively), was operated by Oasis Cinemas, a company created in 1986 (which we have previously come across in connection with the Gate Cinema, Notting Hill) until it transferred to City Screen Ltd in 2004.

Palladium

Architectural flights of fancy

Crossing over from the Oval and onto the bustling star of Brixton Hill, the Palladium Theatre, later the Palladium Picture Theatre, is the penultimate 'SW' visitation. Known as The Fridge, a nightclub and bar since June 1985, the actual origins of the structure date back to the early months of 1913. Its present bland façade is a faceless affair in the heart of the district, deftly overshadowed by the commanding Lambeth Town Hall standing next to it. A photograph purportedly showing the exterior of the building is featured in *The Amber Gazetteer of Suburban London Cinemas*, but it is not, however, in anyway similar to what is now on view. An imposing archway entrance, complete with a dome, had an ABC logo positioned on its tiny balcony above, with ornate windows and false pillars giving emphasis to a visually stimulating exterior. ABC did not take charge of the cinema until October 1963; however, reconstruction work on its frontage did occur after the closure of the building in April 1956. This was prior to its reopening as the 1,156-seater Regal Cinema (878 seats in the stalls and the remainder up in the gallery). Could this then explain the disappearance of these architectural features? Or could it, like the Ritzy in the late 1970s/early '80s, have had its ornamental façade buried beneath plain, dull concrete as is seen today?

Internally, its Rococo styled ceiling was removed as part of a major overhaul in the early 1980s. Entrepreneur Spencer Style owned the Palladium in 1982 in the days when its outward visage was highlighted by fey, Art Nouveau (yet at the same time wondrously 1970s in style too) rainbow type shapes around its main entrance. These have now either been removed or lost beneath the greyness that greets present day club-goers. Something that does look to have survived the onset of time has been the cinema canopy above the centralised entry area.

October 1977 saw an independent company take control of the ABC, as it was then, reopening as the Ace Cinema but closing in March 1981. In the early 1980s, a scheme was devised to bring the Ace back to life; reggae performers such as Aswad had already been gigging here during this period and a new proposal was made to remove half of the 1,200 cinema seating to allow a roller-skating rink to be fitted into the ground floor. A total

The Palladium Cinema, Brixton, currently The Fridge.

of 250 stall seats and 350 gallery seats would be retained for cinema patrons and concert-goers, and the spring of 1982 was penciled in for the cinema section to be up and running. EMI had removed the projectors after the building had been sold and only the cinemascope screen remained.

Somewhat puzzlingly, a local journalist named Cedric Potter, then writing in the *South London Press*, described the look of the building as 'rather like an overgrown toilet'. No changes were made, however, and London's largest privately-owned nightclub made the defunct picture house its home in the summer of 1985.

Pyke's Cinematograph Hall

Montagu's curio

We arrive now at our final destination, Pyke's Cinematograph Hall. Having passed the rejuvenated Ritzy Cinema followed by the Lambeth Town Hall and Fridge nightclub, both on the right-hand side, continue walking along the start of the heavily congested road towards Brixton Hill, where the grubby façade of Mr Pyke's 1910 theatre can be unearthed. Business began on 10 March 1911 and concluded on 10 August 1957 with a sci-fi Western entitled *Beast of Hollow Mountain* (1956) as its main feature. Additional names for this narrow and decidedly compact picture house have been the Clifton and

Pyke's Cinematograph Hall, Brixton, currently a camping shop.

New Royal. In the 1990s, however, it progressed (or its original entrance has) into becoming the home of the Tarpaulin & Tent Manufacturing Company. It housed the business for more than twenty years after formerly presenting itself as a sporting goods store. The building is currently derelict.

Its moulded, blancmange-like frontage is in the form of a half-dome, with three thin windows complimented by two circular ones positioned on either side of its exterior above the entrance. Disappointingly, all have been blocked up, but in exploring a photograph of the cinema captured in the 1940s, one realises that nothing has drastically changed in relation to either the structure of the picture palace or the buildings around it. Projecting out from the head of the domed roof was the New Royalty name, and to me, 'Camping Centre' fails to muster the same sense of curiosity. Stepping inside the cinema before the last business vacated it, moulded leaf plasterwork on the ceiling gave a hint of days gone by, though not particularly flattered by the subsequently cracked and ageing walls all around.

There is not a great deal of detailing to arouse our interest, and around the side street next to the cinema, the establishment of a new housing complex has resulted in the rear of the picture house being lost. The New Royalty/Clifton does warrant a brief visit if only to provide a stimulating contrast with Pyke's other picture palace in Shepherd's Bush which, being slightly larger in scale than the Brixton house, is another equally inviting curio in the story of Montagu A. Pyke.

14

Stratford

The best aspect of Stratford, so the saying goes, is the train station leading back out of it. The devilishly glass constructed train/tube station terminal does have more of a tendency of resembling an anonymous European airport rather than an East London station!

Stratford Rex Cinema

'A very Mediterranean interpretation'

Quaint, yet with its brickwork unattractively coloured in blue, red and peach, the Grade II listed Theatre Royal presented its first cinematographic exhibition in 1887 but never became a consistent home for films. At the time of writing, the Theatre Royal was being given an extensive overhaul with work having progressed through its early stages. The daintiness of the theatre is rudely contrasted with the ultra modernity of the new Stratford Picture House, a multiplex complex enticing patrons with 'stadium seating and massive screens', standing opposite a slight 120-year-old Salway Road elder.

George Coles, the architect of whom we shall hear more in a minute, has another connection with this area other than with the Rex Cinema, located on the High Road. Coles was the architectural might behind the Broadway Super Cinema which stood on Tramway Avenue, across the way from the main shopping centre and very near the Rex. The Broadway was completed in 1927 for Hyams & Gale, and had a seating capacity of 2,768, marking it out as the largest picture house in Britain at the time. Closure came in 1960 and, after brief spells as a factory and a gym, it remained in a derelict state for sometime only for it to be demolished.

A collection of cinemas, in addition to those mentioned, have all failed to survive in the area over the prevailing years: names such as the Palladium, the Empire (hit by a bomb during the Second World War), Gale's Bioscope and the Imperial are now only to be found in a deceased registry. The Cecil Masey-altered West Ham Electric Kinema (opened in 1924) came under the protective arm of Granada Theatres in 1933 and the cinema structure is still standing upright along West Ham Lane, thanks to (or in spite of) a conversion to bingo in the early 1960s. Its façade has been extensively boxed with very little of intrigue left for a picture house now more commonly-known as a Gala club than a cinema theatre. Perhaps of more interest is the Grove Picture Theatre, where film-goers were treated to a free cup of tea back in 1910, when Ernest Brown

The Stratford Rex Cinema.

ran the house, and which must have come as a novel (and rather welcoming) surprise to many of his 400 patrons. Mr Brown's shadow had disappeared from the Grove by the 1920s, at which point the shell of the building was altered to allow talking pictures to be viewed and heard. Within the early months of the 'phoney war' in 1939, the Grove Park Theatre fatefully failed as a moving picture house. It was commandeered as a factory at a later stage and its seemingly unaltered exterior is now derelict. An external pay box can be observed at the Grove premises, although any sign of its existing usefulness remains uncertain.

Nevertheless, we are in Stratford primarily to seek out the Rex Cinema at the far end of the bustling High Street. Its creation came in the form of the 3,000-seater Borough Theatre in August 1986, making it one of the biggest in the country. Both the Borough and Theatre Royal were owned by Alfred Fredericks and it was his company that paid for both theatres to be adapted to enable films to be shown in 1910. March 1933 saw the conclusion of the Borough as a working theatre after it was purchased by Essell Cinemas, with George Coles engaged as its architect. The auditorium was modified and its front at the corner entrance crisply modernised and returned to its glorious splendour after falling into a dreadful state in the 1980s. Bonfire night of 1934 saw the resurgence of the Rex; with 1,889 seats, two cafés and the installation of a Wurlitzer organ brought over from a theatre in Ohio, America, all adding to a terrific new package. In September 1934, the cinema was re-titled the ABC Rex, only for its flagging fortunes to be tempered with the arrival of Cinemascope in 1958. The Wurlitzer, housed in the orchestra pit, was covered up and abandoned as a consequence of the poorly conceived actions. Cinemascope failed to keep a hold on dwindling audience numbers and at the start of November 1969, the ABC Rex screen fell silent.

As fortune would decree, the arrival of the Star bingo club meant that the Wurlitzer was released from captivity and played on occasion once more. Bingo lost its precarious grasp on the building in April 1974, a point from which the fortunes of the Rex took a turn for the worse for a great many years. It was unused for a while prior to its being used for a short time as an Asian cinema, though, from 1975, no further films of any kind would be screened again. A fire bug struck at the heart of the empty hall and following this, the building slipped into decay and dereliction. In 1989, the cinema was in a serious state of abandonment, as a photograph of its crumbling façade given to the author during research into the venue so demonstrated.

As for more recent years, the good news is that the Rex has come back to life, only now as a themed music nightclub with a variety of DJ's in residence each week. Its outer shell has been spruced up and is in a splendid condition for its age. High above the curved concrete corner main entry point, the old Rex name has made a return. Yellow speckled stone stucco is juxtaposed with green metal window frames; viewed from Bridge Road, it shows stone detailing featuring a figure head cast in a semi-circle, enhancing an otherwise plain area. The extent of the damage or changes made internally are not known but still, the Rex has received a new lease of life after a precarious past.

Poster advertising a concert at the Stratford Rex Cinema.

15

Tooting

The Granada Tooting

'You will love Granada. Say Green-ah-da for Granada'. (1931 press campaign for the cinema)

The fun-seeking public of Tooting had a deeply-rooted affection for the smoky beam of light, richly demonstrated by an audience's insistence to remain watching *How Green Was My Valley* one time when a fire broke out in the building, until the police succeeded in vacating the premises.

With a Union Jack fluttering majestically above its Upper Tooting Road veneer (along with the neighbouring Classic), the Mayfair Cinema demonstrated itself somewhat spectacularly across the span of its commercial life. Curtailed in 1919, this was a picture house oddly transposed into a banking establishment and afterwards, an all-pervasive snooker hall. The Mayfair was one of five theatres in the district, all of which, barring the Granada (in the package of a bingo hall), are defunct.

Once situated among the shops in the High Street, the Vogue Picture Palace has long ago been levelled, as has the Astoria on Mitchum Road. Commonly nicknamed the 'A' by the end of the Second World War, its projectors fell silent and its seats were vacant in 1970, closely followed by demolition.

Happily, with such a bountiful expanse of detailing to feast upon, it is difficult to know where to begin in recounting the astounding South London dream house know as the Granada Tooting. Granada Theatres' owner, Sidney Bernstein, came up with the company name after returning from a walking holiday in Andalusia, in southern Spain; a typical luxury for the affluent at a time when the ordinary person had no chance of savouring such delights, but for whom the pictures could transport to foreign climes, albeit for only an evening. Rendering of the Granada building officially commenced in August 1930, yet with planning proposals and rejections all being considered, completion work came closer to three years. *Kine Weekly* (10 September 1931), the foremost trade paper, was there to record the Granada's first night:

> At 7 p.m., sixteen trumpeters blew a fanfare from the steps of the brilliantly lighted façade. At the conclusion . . . there was driven on stage a baby Austin, the doors of which were opened by two of the most stalwart commissionaires. From the car stepped forth a dainty kiddie [who was] presented with a bouquet by a diminutive page and then declared the theatre open.

As a structure, the Granada Tooting, on the junction of Tooting Broadway and Mitchum Road, certainly emits a feeling of a manifestly municipal kind, as did its unusually creamy artificial stone exterior which, in 1931, set the cinema apart from others (as did the introduction of an exterior vertical sign, popular in America but rare for its time in the UK). However, its towered frontage confounds when seen in relation to the interior. The two are diametrically opposed although, somehow, it gels together in a way that is difficult to define.

It was architect Cecil Masey whose adaptation of an earlier work for the Phoenix Theatre in Charring Cross Road, devised by Sir Giles Gilbert, was instead used for the Granada. Massey had seen his own proposal for the structure, modern in styling, rejected by Bernstein in preference of the Scott blueprint. Nonetheless, the exterior does have an effectiveness for which its scale and four-pillared focal point can begin to be acknowledged. A collection of four sour-looking faces grimace from the column peaks, while ample lighting – in the shape of large bulbs – curves around the underside of the canopy, enticing the passer-by to step inside.

The reputation of interior theatre designer Theodore Komisarjevsky weighs heavily at the Granada Tooting, where his work is widely regarded as being the pinnacle of his career. The audacious and eclectic kaleidoscope presentation was formulated while he was a resident in Paris and the princely sum of £500 was received for his solution which, almost eighty years later, is still able to stupefy with its essence of varying medieval and Gothic forms.

Entering into a narrow foyer, cinema-goers would have been met by four pay boxes, two on either side, from which to purchase tickets. Nowadays, Gala bingo players approach the boxes on the right-hand side, while the others opposite have been blocked

The Granada Tooting.

Close-up of the Granada Tooting façade.

up. Almost immediately, the significance that the natural and artificial light plays in developing a sense of atmosphere can be seen, as can the way mirrors are used to suggest a greater depth in the foyer and elsewhere. 'It's a very Mediterranean interpretation', voiced a visitor at an Open House event, in which the Granada is a regular participant. The space is softly lit, while low panels of ornamental wood, reminiscent of red and white poles found outside some barber shops, wrap themselves around the five sets of double doorways taking patrons into the main vestibule.

Measuring much larger than the initial foyer, the main vestibule is striking; an abundance of wood culminates with a larger chandelier in the centre of the room while others have been positioned alongside. A staircase directly in front of the journeyman flows up onto a terrace and onwards towards the circle. Lasting until well into the late 1960s, a sweets kiosk was situated in the middle of the marble floor until it was removed. Antiquated silver 'one arm' bandit machines, brought in by the bingo owners, appear oddly redundant around the hallway. And originally, a second stairway, just above the main entrance and now disused, led to the cinema restaurant which had its own entry point in neighbouring Mitchum Lane. Those enjoying a meal could nonchalantly watch the cinema-goers below queuing to enter the main auditorium; a space that could hold up to 500 patrons at any given time. This is a suitable position from where to notice the wall detailing of the lofty vestibule. The elongated body of mythical griffins are symbolic examples of the rhythm of the theatre, fusing a verse with a hypnotic hook possessing such temerity that the receiver cannot fail to breathe a sigh in astonishment. This is where the audacity of the cinema is clearly in excess, especially from the circle leading down towards the stage, with the extent of the varying styles fused by Komisarjevsky. Volunteers thought that the artist was unable to contain himself, firing off at all angles and causing bewilderment to the viewers.

On the terrace, a sense of anticipation is raised upon reading a sign indicating the 'hall of mirrors' and by swiftly turning left and right, it comes into view. 'It's like a cathedral', marvelled a first-time visitor, as your eyes try to take in the vision presenting itself. A purposely low-level patterned ceiling with a mass of three-quarter length mirrored segments is set off by twin candlesticks in front, which actually work in supplying light, feeling like an apt setting for a Hitchcockian scene. After leaving the glimmering hall, and turning right, one gains a fantastic impression of the general auditorium from the perspective of the circle. Komisarjevsky raises the dramatic atmosphere to such a theatrical degree of eagerness that the new arrival has the sense of a boxer about to enter the arena, as the star of the main event of the evening. It's exciting to ponder what pleasures are to be discovered next and the Granada produces such a sensation over and over again.

Bernstein believed that the public of the 1930s did not necessarily buy a ticket for a specific film but rather for the theatre's sense of occasion and splendour far removed from everyday living. And for patrons back in that difficult time, let alone for the contemporary bingo players, the Tooting Granada would have been confounding.

Coming out onto the circle area, after the appetising hall of mirrors, we find our main course considerably more fulfilling. A coffered ceiling overwhelms, and further chandeliers and candelabras adjourn the yellow tiled walls. By stepping into either of the two exits, we see they are disguised as oriental style, roof-topped abodes; reality strikes when one finds oneself in a stark, modern exit. Hastily returning, the circle begins to articulate itself; everything is on show, presented in such a way that the nearer the eye moves towards the balcony edge, the greater the thought occurs.

American action hero John Wayne, who visited the Granada in 1951.

While describing such cinemas as those created for the Astoria circuit, otherwise categorised as *atmospherics*, Julian Leatheart labelled them 'inside-outs'. This is a useful term to extend to the cathedral-like Granada. Painted arches on each side of the balcony reveal an abundance of immaculately rendered troubadours and damsels by Vladimir Polunin, after adaptation from smaller originals by Leslie le Blond. (Alex Johnstone has also been accredited to the work.) A high volume of wood and metalworking has been retained with a strong feature being the intricate metal railing at the rear of the balcony. Here moreover, each one of the circle seats still has its traditional ashtray on the back; the instalment of the numbers game meant that all seating had been transposed in favour of unsightly booth-type arrangements. But from the stalls, turning towards the circle, its curved balcony edge spanning an area of some 123ft in depth x 68ft wide, has now been occupied by Gala and, disgracefully, the Wurlitzer is said to be entombed under what is now the callers' podium. Back in the formative years of the 1930s, before the introduction of variety acts (arriving in 1934), the only type of music played at the Tooting Cinema was provided by an organist or grand pianist. This all changed soon after, with acts including a festive circus troupe (complete with elephant) and Walthamstow's own Charles Manning, the fondly-recalled conductor, in residence here in late 1933 and early 1934. One performance for a Christmas day radio broadcast found the entire auditorium empty but for the performing musician.

American movie star John Wayne called in at the Tooting Granada in 1951 and was met by a team of usherettes, each beautifully turned out in an orange cape, pillbox hat, puffed silk blouse and blue slacks set off by dark, shiny shoes. Dwindling audience numbers at the end of the 1970s placed the future of the Granada in peril, with sometimes as few as a dozen film-goers sitting in the 3,000-seater hall. A disgruntled Bernstein wanted the theatre demolished and the site redeveloped. However, his wishes were, thankfully, not granted and the building was saved from destruction by a 1972 listing. 'Due to lack of public support this cinema is now closed', decreed the notice outside the Granada in November 1973. That was the last of the celluloid dreams once consumed so feverishly at the cinema, while bingo arrived in 1976 and has remained ever since.

16

Waltham Forest

The London Borough of Waltham Forest is actually made up of four separate areas: Chingford, Leyton, Leytonstone and Walthamstow. Collectively, there have been close to thirty picture houses competing to take the change from the pockets of the local community, but in the 1970s, a distressing 75 per cent of formally operative cinemas in the borough had been erased, and by the new millennium, the Cecil Masey-created Walthamstow Granada was the only working cinema. Some of the others have been demolished, converted to stores, snooker and bingo clubs or, as in the case of our first port of call, the Empress Cinema, left in a state of wretched abandonment.

Waltham Forest is a community where the people are renowned for their steadfastness: not even the terrifying German VII bombs could deter residents from visiting their local films. The severity of the threat posed by the horrific bombs was to create a more tangible concern than the effect of the 1940–1 Blitz, and a number of cinemas suffered as a direct consequence.

The Plaza Cinema

'This wonderful new entertainment'

Bedraggled film advertising boards now enmeshed into a collage show that this crumbling cobweb ghost of a building was once a functioning light in Walthamstow. Its pillared, brick and white slated roof saw its final incarnation as the Cameo Cinema in January 1961 until its final double bill, *Frankenstein* and *Dracula* on 26 January 1963. The cinema, at 468–74 Hoe Street, is very easily missed, vacuously positioned at the far end of the main road and near to the right turning which takes you onto Lea Bridge Road (a journey we shall shortly make to visit the George Coles-generated Savoy). The Plaza is found in the opposite direction to the Granada Cinema and although strangely defined as being in Leyton, Walthamstow tube station is a ten minute walk from the theatre. The Cameo is a picture house most pleasingly remembered for its time under the Plaza bannering, which came about in 1931 and ceased in 1961 when the Cameo title arrived. Its commercial life saw a domino-like list of re-titlements, beginning its life as the Empress, the Scala and, finally, the Cameo.

Conversion to its cinema use dates back to 1909, although conflicting reports mention that it came to be managed by the Good brothers, a family builders merchants, in 1913. This was a result of the same company owning both the Scala (Plaza) and Empire Cinema, sitting in Bell Corner, at the end of Hoe Street. The Empire was consistently advertised in the *Walthamstow Independent* back then but the Scala never was. Rivalry was fierce and each circuit would promote their cinemas as the best thing since sliced bread; the Scala and Empire both offered free admission for any youngster accompanying a paying adult. The Goods were responsible for not only the Cameo Cinema but others too, starting with the Queen's (again in Hoe Street) followed a couple of years later with the Empire and the Empress Electric Picture Theatre House, also known as the Cameo in 1913.

A total of 827 seats (twenty-one in the balcony and 615 in the stalls) were readily made available, in addition to an already healthy number of houses in the vicinity. The company was granted a licence to allow a further eighty patrons to stand at the rear of the auditorium. Following the new Plaza name in 1931, ownership of the building transferred two years later to another local company, Amusements (Leyton) Ltd, a business superceded at the cinema by Clavering & Rose in 1937.

If a throng of excessive cinema-goers managed to squeeze in through the entrance hall, they would pay the ticket cost at a centrally-mounted pay box fully equipped with the latest, four-way automatic ticket machinery. By the time the Plaza came up for sale in 1949, film-goers were being charged an admission of either 1s 5d for the stalls or 1s for the balcony.

During the winter months of 1961, the Plaza was re-titled the Cameo, only for the Cameo Cinema Group to announce in the local press in 1963 that they were closing immediately, to enable its restructuring into a bingo club to be hurried through. In Leyton, advertisements showed the area's first bingo and social club (at the old Savoy Cinema) with a £100 jackpot to lure eager punters in. The present then looked a little shaky for the Bell Corner Cameo Cinema too, promoting itself as 'Walthamstow's best independent release cinema' combining a double bill of 'X' rated films, their adverts declaring, 'for every adult this is it!'

The Plaza Cinema, Waltham Forest.

The Savoy Cinema

'Service with courtesy' (1930s cinema slogan)

Moving on from the melancholy of the Plaza, we now head towards Leyton and to Lea Bridge Road, where this George Coles-designed Savoy Cinema greets us. As the architect professed in the June 1930 edition of *Cinema Theatre & Allied Construction*:

> The cinema elevation should possess dignity and sobriety sufficient to denote its importance, a touch of gaiety for preference; perhaps something dramatic but not too starling; and most telling of all, there should be a powerful attractiveness that will entice us to enter.

I wonder what he would make of his creation nearly nine decades on. The Savoy is a cinema that is certainly showing its age; spikes of foliage sprout forth from the peak of its once proud but now arthritic façade. Its weathered exterior, found in a part of London where the roads are permanently congested, includes a number of shops on either side of its corner positioned entrance, half of which are difficult to ascertain if they are open or closed. The impression suggested to the passer-by is of dereliction. The Savoy has, in fact, been a Gala bingo club for more than twenty years and it is used as the Chances bingo club.

Bingo devotees are confronted by a selection of dazzlingly tawdry electronic gaming machines in the foyer, before they make their way into a second foyer, and eventually into the auditorium. It is here that they can take their positions at any one of the American-style diner seating spaces. Alas, all the authentic stalls seating has been removed, and now there is ample room between each block, but not a cinema-goer in sight. The circle is infrequently called back into use for the bingo patrons, perhaps once a week if there is an especially busy evening or the possibility of a big jackpot. Mainly, it stays darkened. It is a shame because all its rows of cinema seating are intact; its 435 cushioned seats were last occupied by film-goers in the 1970s. As for us, we shall make our way upstairs and by gently pushing open one of the weighty, port-holed doors and fill one of the many vacant seats inside. The cinema maintains a small, discreet and unimposing interior, more functional than anything else. Perhaps Leyton was not an area with a reputation for being rich and diverse in architecture in the 1930s, but with the introduction of the Savoy Cinema, local people had something to extol.

Opening on Boxing Day 1928, the Savoy became the latest current cinema in a long line of great pretenders, as the home of the moving image. Its opening day saw 1,750 patrons fill the hall, described as 'being in the English Renaissance style'. The cinema was exclusively built for Hyman Cohen (although it actually started off as a project for Charring Cross Property Co. Ltd) as a cine-variety theatre, charging a general admission of 6d and 1s for the stalls and 1 6d or 2s for the circle.

An organ recital was given by resident Edgar F. Peto, who left the position soon after, and finished with the Mayor of Leyton officially opening the new cinema. The Savoy would have many resident organists over the coming years, including one named Wharton Trevitt. The edifice was constructed at the tail end of the silent era, though when talkies did arrive, variety acts ceased and the orchestra was dismissed. Variety made a return and cine-variety continued hence forth. The main feature on that first night was *Lost in the Arctic*, beginning after *God Save the King* and the *Pathé Gazette* had been concluded. This was followed by a few stage acts and a musical interlude from Max

Seener and the Savoy orchestra wrapped up proceedings. A short comedy and *Pathé* pictorial segment filled the time prior to the second and final rendition of the National Anthem.

The Savoy was to be the runner-up in showing Al Jolson in *The Singing Fool* (1928), a film which audiences could now *hear* as well as see projected from above their heads. The Carlton Cinema, later the Ace Upton Park, took the honours for being the first to play a talking picture and the King's (on the High Road, Leyton) followed the Savoy two weeks later, with its patrons charged 6*d* and 1*s*. The advancement of the talkies was not lost on the local media, which commented, 'This wonderful new entertainment has found its way to Leyton with lightning rapidity'.

'Locality', acknowledged Coles, a former pupil of Leyton Technical School, 'has a strong bearing on the style and quality of the architecture to be employed . . . a situation in a crowded working-class locality demands a simple and more striking treatment. Good taste in the elevation has now become essential'. This comment could have been referring specifically to this picture house, so apt is the description. The theatre had its own refreshment lounge and issued a monthly programme guide given away free to patrons. It included such gems as the following thoughts made by Maurice Cheepen, a man with a story to tell of his part in the industry (see the Troxy Cinema, page 45). Cheepen was then house manager of the Savoy: '[We] all hope to learn something which is refreshing and encouraging to their minds, and be able to forget the troubles of the day in an ideal if somewhat improbable world.'

In January 1930, United Picture Theatres (UPT) had the lease to the cinema. The UPT was founded by Isidore Schlessinger, a wily South African with nine London picture

The Ace Cinema, Upton Park.

palaces (rising quickly to sixteen), and with cinemas in Clapham Junction, Kilburn, Mile End and Woolwich already under his guidance. The creation of this circuit is significant in the history of cinema circuit distribution, as much as the instigation of the Gaumont-British chain in 1927. By 1928, just in advance of his work on the Savoy, Coles, who was their in-house architect, offered a creative conclusion for two, purpose-built cinemas in the UPT team: the Rivoli in Whitechapel, opened in 1921, and the Stamford Hill Cinema in 1925. All the others in the company were older buildings which had reconstruction plans formulated to upgrade them to suit the growing development of picture houses. (One final cinema was built in 1929, after the Savoy.) UPT was added to the Gaumont Cinema circuit, itself growing into the Rank organisation, after the former incurred drastic financial losses, showing itself in the Savoy being managed by them in 1930. The building was sold for £30,000 and would eventually be re-titled the Leyton Gaumont in February 1950. Gaumont-British, at the time of the Savoy addition to their ranks, had a total of 300 cinemas around the country while the nearest competitor, ABC, had only half of that number. The Odeon circuit finally got its hands on the Gaumont in March 1964 but unusually, the house turned into an independent ownership by 1968 during the harshest period of its life and its identity re-formed as the Curzon Cinema.

Bingo has been played at the Savoy since 1971, when the cinema was known as the Curzon bingo club. The Classic Company had taken control of the building and consequently, the circle was re-opened as the New Curzon Cinema in January 1973 after £55,000 was spent on refurbishment, including seat replenishment and new carpeting. A proposal was made to play contemporary feature films, with late shows combining with screenings of movies taken from the Classic Group's library of 4,000

The Savoy Cinema, Leyton.

titles. Vogue Bingo continued to be played in the stalls. Lamentably, the cinema was brought to an abrupt end in March 1979, while the numbers game was retained. Today, bingo is regularly played at the former Savoy.

Sitting beside, or standing at, the edge of the curling balcony, one feels a sense of cosiness. It is a simple hall, to say the very least, yet it is not without presence. As we cast our attention from the concave ceiling above and down towards the uncomplicated, mezzanine-patterned proscenium arch, now a non-existent stage, its height generates a desire in the heart of the modern guest to have attended a film presentation here.

St James Electric Theatre

The white ghost

In a moment we shall be advancing in search of another picture palace, but before we do so, let us take a brief look at the bottom of the High Street where the 480-seater St James Electric Theatre still stands. Perched next door is St James Street station, which was presumably built after the 1911 creation of the cinema. Steps shaped in a semi-circle are the first indication of its 'pictures' life in an otherwise nondescript structure with only a fancy, plastered frontage giving a pretence of something grander than a brickworked construction. Running down St James Mews, the cinema is a lengthy shape, but one can only imagine what the volume of passing trains must have been like when the building was utilised as a cinema in the late 1930s.

The St James Electric Theatre, Walthamstow, now Abbey Dental Practice.

In 1916 and 1919, the St James Cinema traded proprietors on a couple of occasions and emerged as the Super Cinema for a little while longer. The Regent Cinema was its latest guise in 1930. Shipman & King's circuit had taken to running the house in 1929, yet four years later the cinema closed, in September 1933. It did manage to reopen as the aforementioned Super, under the gaze of Walthamstow Cinemas Ltd, only to flop in this form by February 1934. Its life now playing like a bad 'B' feature, some kind of temporary stability did arrive in November and continued until June 1936 when the doors slammed shut yet again. The year 1938 saw the last attempt at breathing life back into the St James Street Theatre; with regret, it failed. When war broke out, the weekly serial of the building's time as a haphazard cinema was concluded once and for all. But if nothing else, the structure has stood up to the changes that time has necessitated since the curtailment of its cinema days, with a health club and sauna and a dental practice all housed in this white-faced shadow of a picture palace.

Leyton and Leytonstone have each had their ample share of cinemas and the shell of both the Ritz on Leyton High Street and the Savoy on Lea Bridge Road can still be appreciated, if only as a supermarket and bingo club rather than as cinemas. There is not a single other in a long list that has made it through as a modern-day picture house. Leyton casualties number the King's Hall (Century), the Lion Picture Palace and the Markhouse Cinema; the latter a small elevation that closed in 1942, with its frontage rebuilt to accommodate a shop. Meanwhile, in neighbouring Leytonstone, the George Coles revamped Century Cinema (previously the Academy) was demolished in 1983. The Palace Electric Theatre on the High Road had its façade heavily reconstructed in 1955, thus rendering it almost indistinguishable as a cinema; the Rex (later the Leytonstone ABC Bowl), the Gaiety and the Masey/Komisarjevsky Rialto Cinema have all fallen away.

The Premier Electric Theatre

'The cinema for adult entertainment'. (Former cinema slogan outside the building)

Up until 2006, the Churchill snooker and social club provided its members with a choice of ten, full-size tables within the war-torn and seedy environs of East London. Images first exploded across its threshold as the Premier Electric Theatre over the summer of 1910, with its subsequent re-branding as the Premier Talkie Theatre in 1931 and the Savoy Cinema by December 1938. Architects Emden & Egan produced the creative ingredients for a crisp 710-seater hall in 1910, when the picture palace originated as a silent house. It is an economically-charged structure in both height and breadth with its confinements made apparent after walking down the lane at Granleigh Road, just off the High Road, which takes the investigator around the side and back of the building. Today, not a great deal of detailing shows its neon-lit past, a time when the façade possessed the shape of an American Cadillac car or Edward Hopper diner configuration. A night-time photograph of the Savoy can be marvelled at in *Gazeteer of Greater London's Suburban Cinemas* (see Bibliography). Its fabulous contours, which have now been lost, make its derelict state a sad sight.

What must also be mentioned is George Coles' hand in the refurbishment of the theatre in readiness for its reopening in December 1938 as the State Cinema. It took three

The Premier Electric Theatre, Walthamstow, now Churchill's Snooker and Social Club.

months of renovation, consideration and a reduction in capacity to 600 seats for Coles to implement the changes for its latest management, Clavering & Rose. Classic, aerodynamic serpentine windows wrapped around its exterior tower re-invigorated the style of the old Premier, ably enhanced by a dorsal finned sign overflowing from the top of the roof, but incredibly, none of this detailing has remained.

The war years saw the State Cinema close from 1940–43 due to bomb damage and, five years later, the theatre came into the hands of Hyams & Gale Ltd, a familiar name in the cinema business. I have been unable to discover any documentation, but believe that the cinema was closed by 1955, because it was then the home of Waller Enterprises. By 1958, the house was the head office of Regent Films and bingo with sporadic films (including adult certificate features) reinstated after the picture palace had been in use as a club from 1959. By the late 1990s, the Savoy lacked any sign of architectural merit; a doorway was bricked off towards one end of the façade and entry was through a tiny doorway on the immediate left of the frontage. Its shell was coated in white and an unpleasant green block up to street level. If you look at it today, the great dome segment is where the projection booth was originally situated.

Before I go on to summarise the life of the Dominion Cinema, Buxton Road, Walthamstow, I'll say a brief word or two about the structure demolished to make way for its construction: the former Prince's Pavilion. This elementary hall began exhibiting moving pictures as far back as 1909 and, following alteration work, the site progressed to become Walthamstow's first, purpose-built cinema in 1911/12. This was notable due to the fact that most picture houses at the time were commonly adapted from old roller-skating rinks or shops. Interior embellishment was limited at the Pavilion, with its auditorium being categorised as somewhat sparse. Just as many others had, the cinema here included wooden benches towards the immediate front of the screen which were for the less affluent patrons to occupy. A number of indiscreetly-fixed electrical lamps would be called upon to illuminate the stalls when necessary.

The Dominion cinema

'Come! Come! Come!' (1930s plea to promote the opening of the Dominion)

The Pavilion lasted for twenty years and, after playing an important role in the history of the area, it was demolished and in its place the Dominion Cinema marked its own inauguration on the evening of 22 December 1930. According to local authors J.W. Howes and D. Law in *Shopper's Paradise*, a dense fog that night meant many of the invited guests missed attending a special show officiated by the Mayor of Walthamstow and the Lord Lieutenant of Essex.

'Come! Come! Come!' roared the local press advertisement, to enjoy a 'full all-talking star programme'. Clifford Aish was the architect given the task of visualising a new 300-seater palace where the management promised the best films at a more palatable price than a trip up west. Corners would not be cut and the cinema was to be a prestigious and 'luxurious' hall. Aish was already known for an extensive portfolio of London theatres and across the country, so he would hardly have required the following flattering rhetoric: 'The Dominion Theatre forms an imposing and impressive landmark in Walthamstow and is a building which you can be justly proud'.

A resounding trumpet fanfare started the proceedings on the first night, followed by a second, including pipers of HM Royal Scots Guard. Next came the *William Tell Overture* performed by soloists and resident organist, Rex O'Grady, to set the tone of the show. The supporting feature film was a Douglas Fairbanks Junior dud called *Little Accident* (1930) which had been preceded by solo acts from a baritone and a comedienne. News and sound snippets were followed by a short talkie and then came the main film, *The Storm*, a rugged melodrama starring Lupe Velez. And finally, as if this had not been enough, a good sing-song closed the evening with *God Save the King* and *Auld Lang Syne* played to an appreciative audience.

The Western Electric sound system enhanced a continuous programme aimed at combining talkies with the occasional silent film offered in the programming schedule. Three shows each day would run concurrently from early afternoon through to late evening, with tickets marked at 2s 4d and 1s 6d for the front and rear of the grand circle or at 1s 3d for seating in the front and back stalls. The ABC Dominion came to fruition some three months after the Cecil Masey/Komisarjevsky marvel, the Granada Cinema, in nearby Hoe Street. Competition was immense. Management at the Dominion were particularly keen to stress the positive aspects of their new house, going so far as to mention that its interior design was finished with a 'commendable restraint', thus avoiding, they explained, 'any jazz or garish display which we feel our patrons will appreciate'.

Inside the cinema, an autumnal colour scheme complimented plasterwork decorations inspired by the Renaissance. Regarded as 'charming and simple', this aspect of its make-up was seen as a key requirement for a modern cinema of the 1930s, such as the Dominion. Its oddly-positioned entrance at the side of the building had a series of corridors leading to and from the stalls, while gangways additionally took the patron to a unique component of the cinema; a raised dais (chosen by Aish) instead of the more common circle structuring. If cinema-goers could manage to find their way into the 82ft wide auditorium, via an entrance hall, ample blue and bronzed Italian piers (a pillar arch support) and a lighting pedestal with walnut woodworking, would have welcomed them. The Granada had its Christie organ and here at the Dominion, they had a special

The Dominion Cinema, Walthamstow.

Wurlitzer instrument, freshly purchased and imported from America. Combining a pipe organ and the varying voices of an entire symphony orchestra under the control of a single musician, O'Grady, it was the first such device to grace any local cinema, and a number of recordings were made on it. (In 1958 it was sold to a Northampton company.) O'Grady had brought more than a decade's worth of experience to his appointment as cinema organist and at 28, he had already tickled the ivories in theatres across Britain and America.

Wrestling briefly appeared at the Dominion Cinema in March 1958 after film screening ceased, however public demand calling for its return brought them back by October that year. Films continued being shown until, ironically, a lack of patronage saw to its closure in March 1961 when again, wrestling momentarily reinstated itself.

A rear exit opening out onto an adjacent supermarket shows its bingo signage, while both the Jasmine and Dominion are still fixed in place. A fire in recent years devastated much of this area, with its bulbed, panelled canopy almost melting away. Running parallel with the pedestrianised High Street, the Buxton Road Jasmine bingo club was open as late as 1997. I unearthed a substantial amount of used gaming books in a skip just outside the building accompanied by old signage and a scattering of hand-rendered posters reading, 'Sunday Afternoon Specials – Penny Flyer'. Over the summer months of 1999, a considerable amount of interior renovation work took place in the building, and upon further investigation, I saw floodlights inside, but what I could observe of the auditorium – the stalls at least; seemed little more than a ruin. There was not a single seat or anything else visible and it looked to be in a serious process of being gutted.

The Empire Cinema

'For men only'

In advance of our main presentation, the Granada Cinema, we continue along Hoe Street until the Empire Cinema comes forth. Being less than a five minute walk from the Granada, the Empire is a self-contained building at the junction interchange known locally as Bell Corner. The architect responsible for the cinema remains unknown; however, its life began in February 1913 as an 815-seater theatre, with 600 seats in the stalls and 215 in the balcony. The price of admission was 3*d*, 6*d*, 9*d* and a single shilling. Owned and ran by the Good brothers from 1913, it had its own house orchestra playing tunes from the early evening onwards.

A temporary closure of the cinema in 1933 corresponded with a change in proprietor exhibiting a renewed campaign starting on Boxing Day of that same year, when it recommenced flickering light in the darkness. Life continued at the Empire well into March 1961, known as the new Cameo Cinema; and flopping drastically, it ceased to trade less than six months later. With film product decreasing in creative value as the Empire moved into its sixth decade, the building's use switched to bingo. It began the first game in its new lease of life in the second week of September and would seem to have continued throughout that era prior to its final numbers being called with the resurgence of films in April 1970. Films were still being shown at the Empire in the 1960s but simply on a limited Sunday afternoon engagement; coming into life in 1963, the Apnee Film Society filled a cultural need for Asian members in the community. This was at the time when the home video

The Empire Cinema, Walthamstow, now Rileys American Pool and Snooker Club.

boom of the early 1980s had not yet materialised. Now there exists a generous video/DVD rental and sales market but features still play at the New Curzon Cinema on Turnpike Lane.

The Empire, re-emerging also as the Tattler Film Club, ran consecutively to August 1981 as a venue for playing hardcore sex films with titles such as *Red Hot Lady* and *Sex Mania* indicative of the type of productions being given an airing. A typical programme dating from 1977 demonstrates further: 'True Blue – A programme of two sensational uncensored films FOR MEN ONLY' ran an advertisement to draw punters in, with the price of tickets set at only £1.50.

Its corner entrance looking out onto the busy junction at the end of Hoe Street, its steps leading up are now out of use, and what was once a side exit doorway of the Empire Cinema has turned into the main access point to a snooker club. It is an unfussy elevation which, like the *Doctor Who* TARDIS, is surprisingly larger within than its exterior might at first suggest. Following the cinema's closure, an amusement arcade adopted the building as its home prior to reuse as the Churchill Snooker and Social Club in 1981, boasting eleven full-sized tables. I somewhat doubt the Empire was much of a competitor against the larger Dominion or Granada picture houses located nearby.

The Granada Cinema

'Laughter and smiles with a cheeky word or two . . . ' (Henry Hall, a war-time doorman at the Granada)

We are now ready to explore the main attraction: the Granada Cinema on Hoe Street. Of all the picture houses to have come and gone in Waltham Forest over the last century, including popular names like the King's, Palace Electric, Rex and Rialto, it is the Granada that, up until a couple of years ago, was the sole survivor as a full-time ABC venue.

Commencing on 15 October 1930, the cinema has not continued completely unscathed; its genuine Christie organ was rendered useless as a result of a 1958 creative tantrum by Count Basie, while restructuring of the original auditorium into three small screens has radically altered the Granada. The Victoria Hall had stood on the land prior to the Granada being assembled, with its own doors cast open to a wary populace in 1887. Momentarily calling itself the King's Theatre in advance of a return to its original title in 1907, the cinema would follow on to become Walthamstow's first cinema with a full-time occupancy.

By the time Granada had blasted its way into the minds of local cinema-goers, its architect, Cecil Masey, and interior designer, Theodore Komisarjevsky, had already collaborated on another building in Leytonstone, although the Walthamstow Granada was the first they had both designed, built and decorated for the circuit. The Rialto Cinema, Leytonstone (altered by the team in 1927) had previously been a roller-skating rink, and as a theatre it was a part of the Bernstein circuit, the proprietor being Sidney Bernstein, later Lord Bernstein.

Ticket demand for the gala performance at the Granada had resulted in a lengthy queue forming from midday and stretching along Hoe Street, with people waiting in eager anticipation of the first show. Highlights of the evening came by way of Spanish dancing girls and a musical spot by the resident twenty-piece orchestra led by E.J. Barker. Sandwiched between a Mickey Mouse cartoon and the main screening, a feature called *Splinters* (1929) and an organ recital put a smile on many of the 2,967 faces gathered.

In the ABC Walthamstow, eventually called EMD Cinema, the vestibule had to its right a ticket desk, and in the centre was a sweets kiosk, hidden behind which was the general access down to what would have been Screens 2 and 3. Upstairs, reached by way of a dual staircase, is a spacious terrace complimented by a magnitude of mirrors, and not much else. The main auditorium was described in the 1930s as being Moorish-inspired and 'rich in the sphere of architecture'. A huge expanse, with the screen below looking as if it is far off in the distance, and a single chandelier in the centre of the ceiling with four smaller sized ones around it, begin the intrigue. Watching a film in the circle in the mid-1990s, you could glimpse its glory in the semi-darkness, and the dark, heavy woodworking around the exit ways increased its appeal. Two hugely intricate grilles at either side of the stage have taken attention away from the overwhelming void now left after the removal of all front stalls seating (during tripling). Komisarjevsky's conspicuous reputation as a bombastic fellow could be confounded by his belief that the cinema offered:

> . . . a flavour of romance for which they [the patrons] crave. The richly decorated theatre, the comfort with which they are surrounded, the efficiency of service contribute to an atmosphere and sense of well-being of which the majority have hitherto only imagined.

Writing in the souvenir programme to commemorate the launch of the Walthamstow Cinema, Komisarjevsky reflected upon some of the ideas leading to what was incorporated:

> For the large entrance hall I chose decorations in the seventeenth-century Spanish Baroque style. With the sole intention of creating the atmosphere of Moorish Spain in the up-to-date Granada Theatre auditorium, not in a vain effort to reproduce the medieval Spanish architecture for a museum, but for the interior of twentieth century Hoe Street, Walthamstow.

If you were to see Screen 1, you would understand this description. Bizarrely, cinemagoers also had the pleasure of breathing in part of the six million cubic feet of fresh air circulating into the auditorium every hour by means of a very modern heating system. In the early days, satisfied visitors paid 8d or 1s for the stalls or 1s 6d and 2s 4d for the circle. 'My mother', remembered Irene Duggett in a reminiscence exhibition at Waltham Forest Local History Museum, 'enjoyed the stage show which came in between the two films with the organist rising up from the depths whilst playing. She made a point of sitting between the expensive front stalls and the somewhat cheaper next block'.

From the outset a cine-variety theatre, alternatively featuring films and live shows, the Granada provided excellent facilities for an assortment of top show business names between 1946 and 1973. It would have been a cozy place to play in, both sprawling and still relatively intimate. Truly extensive in range, performers included Jerry Lee Lewis, The Beatles, The Kinks, The Who, Dusty Springfield, the Rolling Stones, The Monkees, Roy Orbison and Dizzy Gillespie, among many others. The contrived antics of P.J. Proby, a fizzing 1960s sensation, caused pandemonium after he split his pants during a live show! But a real crisis occurred in 1958, in the midst of preparations for a show by Count Basie (tickets being 5s and 15s), when he complained of insufficient space for his orchestra, and demanded that the organ be removed from the pit to allow them additional room. This resulted in the apparatus being made inoperative and what followed was that the orchestra pit itself was filled in thereafter. The Christie organ was of such nobility that most Granada cinemas had their own, and in 1985, after years of neglect which rendered the instrument unplayable, it was brought back. A special concert offering, 'an earful of nostalgia' was arranged in the large Screen 1 after extensive restoration work to the organ had proven a success. The sound of the Christie was heard again after too long a silence.

With the quest to find an alternative appeal to aid an already staid product, cinemas looked to such fads as Cinemascope in the 1950s to combat the advent of television. This new format arrived at the Granada in 1954 with the historical epic *The Robe*

The Granada Cinema, Walthamstow.

(1953) being the first to be pulled into focus on the letter-box screen. The cinema was unique in that it was the only one in the locality to have a luxurious four-track magnetic stereo sound; all other halls could only offer mono. Progression had been made from the days of its Western Electric sound installation in the unchartered waters of the late 1920s, of which the then management gloated, 'Guarantees the living voice without mechanical distortion'.

Pressing on into the 1970s, only seven of the original twenty-eight cinemas in the area are left operational. Inevitably, in a theatre the scale of the Granada, parts of its seating were no longer used; a statement to dwindling audiences. Perhaps not too surprisingly, the Walthamstow Granada joined the ranks of others in transforming into a new, three-screen venue in October 1973. Two cinemas were built under the circle and the circle itself formed the home for the remaining screen. On Screen 1, Richard Beckinsale and Paula Wilcox could be seen by 944 cinema-goers, struggling as *The Lovers* (1972), while Screen 2 and 3 played to 181 patrons in each, with *The Poseidon Adventure* (1972) and Stanley Kubrick's infamous *A Clockwork Orange* (1971) respectively. The Granada subsequently made the local news when it was discovered that it had employed the first female manager.

The two Menahems, Golan and Globus of the Cannon Group, purchased what was left of the Granada cinema circuit in the late 1980s, for a total of £3.3 million. Its fractured exterior façade collaborates with its interior, with one only having to look at the shape of the windows above the canopy to see the linkage with the terrace's interior mirrors. The former cinema café area had, in recent times, been the home of the Victoria public house (used as a dance studio before) and within a street that once numbered eight cinemas, the Granada was the last to remain open. Its future is still uncertain and it is cloaked in dereliction.

The Ritz Cinema

'Represents the most modern in cinema architecture . . . the embodiment of the best scientific knowledge and entertainment'

ABC's chief architect W.R. Glen found a 'super' solution for the circuit's latest picture house with the enlistment of the Rio to its ranks on 4 July 1938. With a stalls space containing 1,532 seats and an 886 seat circle capacity, the opening feature premièring there was Cecil B. de Mille's adventure romance *The Bucaneer* (1938) supported by comedic actor Joe E. Brown in *Fit for a King* (1937). The Ritz came to fruition in the same year three new Odeons were planted in Leicester Square, Balham Hill and Bexley, as well as the Warner Cinema in Leicester Square. A matinee admission of 6*d* and 1*s* was levied for the circle and stalls, while evening tickets cost the same for the stalls and 1*s* 3*d* or 1*s* 3*d* for the circle. Supplemented by a manager named F.J. Nash-Sex (a fabulous name right out of an *Austin Powers* spoof!), an emphasis was placed on a high-tech sound facility, in this instance an RCA system. 'The accents and inflections of voice', proclaimed the Ritz hierarchy, 'can be heard as though the artistes were appearing in person, and singing in particularly is clear and beautiful'.

In December 1978, after forty years, the theatre evolved into the Crown Cinema but closure arrived sooner rather than later in December 1979. Late night Kung Fu movies did continue for a few weeks after but soon petered out and the venue was turned over for conversion into a B&Q home maintenance store.

The Ritz façade still looks similar to the way it was in its cinema days, with moulded, sandcastle-like styling containing lots of curved, vertical lines. Its beige faience and concrete upper frontage has one or two hairline cracks, but otherwise has kept a grip of its original purpose, if only in structure. You can find the building easily from the Plaza Cinema in Hoe Street by simply crossing over the junction which takes you onto Leyton's High Road (Lea Bridge Road was the turning right at the Bakers Arms pub). The Ritz is a little way past the William IV public house, where the remains of another picture house can be deciphered in the anatomy of a Poundstretcher shop on the corner of Belmont Park Road. One clue is an actual cinema fire exit which comes out into William Street before St Helier Road takes you behind the side and rear of the cinema. It is here that the stylish High Street veneer gives an impression of being an entirely separate shell in relation to the main body of the house. Many of the cinema windows are now bricked up around the back, where a car park in St Helier Street shows how the original proprietors, ABC, clearly envisioned a high percentage rate of visitors.

Advancing into the foyer, or at least what was once regarded as such, a few plaster accoutrements on the walls are the only symbols of any creative flair, recalling that this was a modern 'super cinema', whereby austerity was the order the day. It is a little bit of a let down after the interest of the façade stirred up some excitement. A staircase on the left and right leading up to a strangely minute doorway gives a peek at its picture house past. Otherwise, the entrance through to the supermarket, presumably once the stalls itself, has a false ceiling and no character whatsoever. Behind the scenes, in non-public access areas, the building belies its past but, unfortunately, we cannot explore such prime locations. However, it is worth taking a look in a neighbourhood with a succession of picture house opportunities to explore, the Ritz being only one of them.

The now direlict Ritz Cinema, Walthamstow.

17

East End Cinemas

It would be remiss not to mention a tumultuous period in the history of the next part of London that we are visiting, and the effect of the Second World War upon the cinemas of Manor Park, Forest Gate, Upton Park and East and West Ham. The first daylight raid on the capital came on 7 September 1940 and one casualty was the Kinema Picture House (it would again be a casualty in 1941 and in 1945, when all of its glass windows were shattered and doors blown off their hinges). In relation to this second incident, despite the fact that its roof had been blown off, astonishingly, some fifty patrons remained in the auditorium watching a musical. Tragically, most of those in attendance would not arrive home that night. The East Ham Granada on Barking Road was struck by bombs on a couple of occasions but was fortunate enough to escape being a direct hit by no more than a fraction. The assistant manager and second projectionist had been on fire watch (all staff were required to take their turn) that evening and were blasted off the roof due to the impact of the explosion. The locales of East Ham, Woolwich, Greenwich, Battersea and Wandsworth suffered intensely from the chilling development of the flying 'V' bombs and rockets; East and West Ham had their share of horrors.

Out of a total of 4,000 cinemas in the UK, 160 were destroyed during the war and a total of sixty of those recorded were London picture houses. The *Luftwaffe* swept mercilessly across Britain on over ninety-nine night-time raids. As bombs rained down, fire engines screeched and ammunition was being fired at the enemy above, audiences persisted in visiting their local cinemas. There was a period where the intensity and fear created by the onset of the raids deterred attendance, but generally people went, regardless of roofs caving in or rain falling into the auditorium. A vivid account of this frightful time is recalled in *Red Roses Every Night – London Cinemas Under Fire* by Guy Morgan.

The Coronation Picture Palace

Twice nightly

A hop and a skip from Woodgrange Park train station, we turn right onto Romford Road where its junction intersects with Forest Drive, and as we take a right at the Earl of Essex pub on the corner, the enormous Coronation Picture Palace comes into view. Moving picture house architect Clifford Aish devised the structure of the now listed

The Coronation Picture Palace, currently Manor Park Snooker Club.

building that in its day could welcome 1,845 cinema-goers. The Coronation was ready to entertain patrons from 28 May 1921 and would do so consecutively for the next seven decades. Its sprawling exterior spreads along the top end of the High Street and, perched high above its pinched entrance, the Coronation name can still be seen. The building is totally intact but unfortunately, its formation has been rendered ugly by a crudely applied canopy installed by the current owners: Manor Park Snooker Club. A hulking great building, its façade contains some genteel detailing beautifully set off by a joyous figure plucking at a harp, itself located beneath the second Coronation name rendering, observed from Crimborne Road which runs along the edge of the cinema.

Since the closure of the picture palace on 23 November 1968, the theatre appears to have remained a vacant lot until the snooker club's installation of thirty full-sized tables in 1985. The snooker club only avails itself of the stalls area and for storage purposes, a limited section of the foyer. Other parts of the general foyer and the entire circle, now devoid of all of its cinema seating (presently being stored in the cellar), are abandoned. A spokesman for the club outlined the difficulties compounded by restrictive structural alterations and safety elements regarding public access to the cinema proving prohibitive. What a shame that this cannot be said for our next venue: the Odeon in Forest Gate.

The Odeon Cinema

'The hallmark of luxury entertainment' (Odeon slogan from the 1930s)

A ten-minute jaunt from the Coronation Picture Palace takes us onto Romford Road, Forest Gate; and to an area known as Princess Alice. The label sprang from the prominence of a public house on the opposite side of the road from the cinema building which we are here to see: the Odeon, a 1937 addition to the company, created by in-house architect, Andrew Mather. At the beginning of March, the 1,806-seater picture house set forth on its community life which, at present, is being used by a mosque and community centre. Odeon, and then Rank, had owned the building right through to its closure on 1 November 1975, when a plan to lure cinema-goers into bingo playing failed miserably. Afterwards, the cinema fell into disuse (the Odeon name stood attached to its frontage until 1995) prior to its stalls section being spoiled through its incorporation into a snooker club. A fake ceiling and an overbearing wooden surround snuffed out any of its former auditorium character, turning it into an anonymous mediocrity. Within the house, after passing through the modernised reception hall and destroyed stalls, one sees the possibilities alluded to, but its exterior demeanor appears anticlimactic. The faded grey/silver-blocked frontage, with light Moslem adornments indicate that beneath the sheen of the mosque, the structure could be as it was. Three façade windows, their frames painted green, form the main centre of attention, with jagged ironwork topped off by green, pod-like effects at the top of the assemblage. The Odeon was purchased in 1994 by the mosque organisation, a foundation with fellow centres in Birmingham, Bradford and Manchester, and which regularly has a thousand attendees.

Patience is required as we endeavor to climb the stairs up to what was the foyer leading to the circle. And what a fantastic transformation: the architect has taken advantage of the natural light from the façade windows to generate a vivacity that makes the space very welcoming. This part of the cinema building is not in use by the proprietors and thus, it is from this point that elements of the original design are

The Odeon Cinema, Forest Gate.

gradually, lamentably revealed. An authentic circle sign placed above the doorway clarifies our whereabouts as we take a left and move up a subsequent flight of winding stairs, which eventually arrives at what I found to be the most distinguishing spot in the building: the circle. Plastering and paint work progressively deteriorate (even the concrete steps have crumbled) in a completely abandoned area where the electricity supply has waned. Row upon row of dusty cinema seating, in addition to the haunted windows of the projection booth, remain, cloaked in darkness and in a state of suspended animation. The sense of atmosphere is immense and is only jeopardized when we learn that there are redevelopment proposals for the entire floor, consisting of flattening the ceiling and replacing the seating. At an overall cost of £2 million, there are evidently no planning restrictions to protect what remains of the essence of Mather's original architecture which its exterior, circle foyer and circle itself, have in abundance. If such a programme is instigated, it would be a great loss if the building's cinema spirit is obliterated to the same capacity that the stalls have been.

Mather's imagination generated original design blueprints for more than thirty Odeon cinemas and his contribution did not go unrecognised by proprietor Oscar Deusch. Speaking after the death of the architect in 1938, he eulogised in *Kine Weekly*, '[His] passing leaves a gap in my organisation which will be hard to fill. His modesty and sincerity', concluded Deusch, 'made him a figure who was beloved by us all'. Let us hope that the building is allowed to sustain a degree, however slight, of his sensitivity in the future.

Carlton Cinema

'These places of entertainment gave lives a touch of luster and gaiety which they stood in great need.' (Audrey Field in Picture Palace)

This was a picture house that ended up as forerunner to another George Coles Egyptian-influenced façade, the Carlton in Islington. The similarities are many, predominantly with the use and styling of ornate central supporting pillars and exterior cornice pattern work.

The Carlton was built on an area that was once a school, and Coles maintained a part of the former structure in the form of the new picture palace. The Carlton could hold 2,117 people in a building that was commissioned by Clavering & Rose, a company that already owned twenty cinemas in their circuit, as the Upton Park Cinema (its original name) became their latest on 29 October 1928. It was the first picture palace outside of the West End, and only the fifth in the country to successfully switch over to talking pictures.

With the Great Depression soon to reach its peak, competition for staff vacancies at the modern cinema was intense and more than 200 applied. A team of twenty-eight usherettes serviced the auditorium, with the management stipulation that suitability for the job entailed staff to be 5ft 4in tall, so that the 'pretty, mini-skirted uniforms would fit everybody'. Management at the theatre cared about their customers and the importance of taking them away from their problems (for an evening at least). 'The seating capacity at the Upton Park', said Chas H.V. Brown, its first house manager, 'was 2,100. One night I managed to accommodate 9,000'. Coles designed the theatre in the manner of a stadium-type auditorium, thus allowing variety performances to be delivered on stage, alongside the regular film scheduling. A Compton organ was housed in the theatre to compliment the daily 2 p.m.–11 p.m. picture shows that cost 6d and 1s for the stalls and 1s 6d or 2 for the circle.

The Upton Park changed its name to the ABC in February 1936 and would entertain local audiences for the next four years, at which time disaster struck in the form of a German bombardment in September 1940. This was not the only time the theatre was closed due to bomb damage; with the war in Europe almost won, January 1945 saw the ABC severely affected by one of the thirty-six flying bombs (and twenty rockets) that struck the neighbourhood during hostilities. A V2 rocket demolished the captivating and defining Egyptian stylized façade and it was never the same again. The ABC Carlton Cinema reopened in August 1953 following restoration work by architect C.J. Forester, which reduced the seating capacity to 1,755. Further woe came with the construction of a modern, nondescript façade. A new foyer was also brought forth, and this area is the home of a greengrocer's today. The cinema established itself as a part of Carlton Terrace, with a row of flats and shops above completing the scheme. The latter have both remained but where the auditorium was, a car park is now situated where this intrinsic heart of the building would have been found. Meanwhile all that has survived of the cinema frontage is its distressed canopy, all battered and debris-like, among the busy produce stores that prosper around it.

Earlier on in September 1961, the ABC Carlton became the ABC, flickering on into November 1978, after which time Alternative Cinema Entertainments took charge of the old cinema. It was ready for its next phase as a working picture house by February of the following year and ran as such until a Mel Gibson double bill of *Mad Max I & II* came to be its final film showing on 23 March 1983.

The Boleyn Electric Theatre

'The cinema is primarily a sort of public lounge . . . an optical lucky dip'.
(P. Morton Shand, The Architect of Pleasure)

Writing in *Cinemas of Essex*, an expansive pictorial gazetteer, author Bob Grimwood alludes to the fate of the East Ham Odeon cinema being met with destruction in 1994. As fortune would have it, conflicting evidence points to the fact that this Barking Road picture house, a stone's throw from the Granada, is actually in operation as a healthy, full-time Asian house called the Boleyn Cinema. As an 800-seater auditorium, the Boleyn Electric Theatre was opened in October 1910 by H.H. & S.R. Dartnall and continued on well into the 1920s. The skills of Cecil Masey were called on to negotiate a series of necessary changes to enable the installation of sound equipment, along with a fresh new canopy, while a change of name to the New Boleyn Cinema rounded off the scheme. The Boleyn Electric Cinema became its newest moniker in 1932, yet in 1936, Odeon had purchased the site with the sole intention of constructing their own cinema, which they duly did.

The vivacious and improved Odeon Cinema, found next to the Boleyn pub, on the corner of Green Street where it flows onto Barking Road (close to West Ham United's football ground), opened on 18 July 1938 with a 2,212 seating capacity. Modernised by Keith P. Roberts of Andrew Mather's practice, its pale blue façade almost presents itself as a cold forerunner of the governmental office buildings of the 1960s, combining

The Boleyn Electric Theatre, East Ham.

vertical, orderly lines in a cool but functional presentation not especially akin with the glitzy bedside companion of the movies. It is not without artistic merit, even when acknowledged in the context of modernity: an appealing part of the exterior can be seen on the underside of the façade roof, where a grouping of almost seventy small lights creates a spaceship-like feel to the form. The Odeon name once ran right across the top of a large window above the entrance, set off by strips of vertical metalwork. As well as being positioned here, the circuit identity was also planted on the side insets of the frontage which today has the Boleyn Cinema name on a vertical banner.

The movement of pictures finally ceased on 31 October 1981, with Disney's *Sleeping Beauty* providing the epitaph. An attempt to make the theatre the home of bingo in the late 1980s proved unsuccessful, although permission seems to have been granted. Pictures with an Eastern flavour now glisten here, and the foyer as it stands now looks to be in a very reasonable condition. A glimpse of a wall mural beneath the circle staircase looked very atmospheric and reminiscent of a similarly stylized work at the Finsbury Park Astoria.

The Granada Cinema

'At your service' (Cinema slogan)

While on Barking Road, we visit the last two cinemas on our itinerary, which are now both well-established bingo clubs – the Gala (formerly the Granada) and the Mecca (originally the Premier Electric) on the adjacent High Street. Both have strong links with the Granada circuit too. Bingo first cast its shadow across the Granada on a permanent basis in January 1976, some time after concerts and Asian film shows had run their course. The concluding feature shown here on 1 November 1974 was the nostalgia-fest *That'll be the Day*.

When we return to its 1914 beginnings, we discover an interesting fact: the Granada was not the first theatre to stand on this site, rather the East Ham Empire Kinema was. In the 1920s, the prolific development of talking pictures meant that many picture houses were unable to cope. So to compete with the other houses, the Empire was briefly closed to allow the necessary re-wiring for talkies in order to sustain the possibility of commercial longevity. It fell to George Coles to see through the remodelling in 1929 and a new Chrisitie organ became its latest acquisition in a period of great change within the industry. Architect W.S. Trent has also been recorded as being responsible for further alterations to the structure in the following year as Komisarjevsky has been for the interior. The Boleyn Theatre evolved from the changes, but, unfortunately, this tale does not have a happy ending as the theatre was flattened to allow the arrival of the new kid on the block, the Granada Cinema.

Renaissance in style, the cinema could accommodate 2,648 patrons, though its history has not always been calm: Trent had a major disagreement with Sidney

The Granada Cinema, East Ham, now Gala Bingo.

Bernstein (owner of the Granada circuit) as he had proposed a modern-looking auditorium which was rejected by Bernstein. He himself chose Komisarjevsky's proposal and Trent was furious, so much so that he demanded a clear distinction be made that he was not responsible for the interior design at this Granada. Unexpectedly, the Christie organ was replaced by a Wurlitzer at the new cinema, which presented its initial programme of features on 30 November. The Second World War made itself known at the Granada with German raids in 1942 and 1944, the latter seeing three flying bombs detonate very near the theatre, consequently resulting in its closure for three weeks. On a more positive note, live acts proved to be very popular in the 1960s and made the venue an extremely well-attended destination for locals.

Owned by Gaumont-British but controlled under Bernstein Theatres, the Granada was to close in 1974 for bingo purposes until 1992, when the building was taken over by Bass and renamed the Gala. Its lovely, curved magnolia and blue façade with steps leading into the entrance hall, presents a dominant E6 landmark. Its foyer is initially a disappointment; littered with an abundance of mirrors and an excess of gaming machines. It is a risible environment only salvaged by a hint of what once was: a twinkling of Komisarjevsky's alluring décor and a balcony with a vaulting, barrelled ceiling disclosing its former intent.

The Premier Electric Theatre

There were loads of cinemas in the East Ham locality

We conclude our exploration with a stroll to East Ham's High Street North and to the Premier Electric Theatre. The Premier was given a new modern façade by Granada shortly after the opening of the nearby namesake, a mere half a mile away, and the Premier was added to the East Ham collection in 1912. During the inter-war years, West Ham alone had nineteen cinemas, the Granada had been unable to play Gaumont releases because the Premier had them as well as competition from the ABC chain, while in July 1938, the arrival of the new East Ham Odeon made it even more difficult for both to exist. So the Granada was confined to playing independent pictures, with live shows helping to support it financially along with the introduction of Cinemascope in the 1950s. Architects Ewen & Barr conceived the modelling for the picture house but little could they have realised that their cinema would, in 1921, be converted into forming the basis of an entrance, foyer and café for a new, larger dream house. The Premier Super opened its doors on 12 March 1921 with a patron capacity of 2,409 (2,118 has also been purported). W.R. Trent converted the old building, with a bigger theatre constructed at the rear to include new stage facilities, dressing rooms and orchestra pit with a specially-built organ, all set to placate local cinema-goers. Premier Super Cinemas ran the picture house before its passing to the PCT circuit and then, in 1927/8, it came under the guardianship of Gaumont-British.

Following the 1945 conclusion of the war in Europe, the Premier Cinema, as it was then titled, was absorbed into the Rank Organisation by 1948 and renamed the Gaumont. The Gaumont was added to the Odeon circuit at the start of the 1960s, and was closed and then replaced by bingo in April 1963, as it has remained since. Top Rank procured the Mecca chain of bingo halls in 1977 and after conducting extensive

The Premier Electric Theatre, East Ham, now Mecca Bingo.

market research, the company decided to maintain the Mecca name for all its halls. At this Mecca, the High Street frontage, in a non-pedestrianised area, looks out of synch with the interior; a black tower façade acts purely as a front. The building is a low-level, extended shape that brings about a somewhat diminutive expectancy, but upon entering the auditorium, this is not the case. The cinema projection has apparently been left intact since taking its final breath in the 1960s. Seating in the picture house circle has been replaced by the bingo company and now an ample 1,800 seats can be found in the old stalls and circle. Both the stage and cellar are currently put into use as a bar and stock room respectively.

18

Woolwich

'There used to be six cinemas in Woolwich; now there are none left.' (David Johnstone, local resident)

Ambling out from North Woolwich train station and turning right, the towered entrance to the Woolwich–Greenwich foot tunnel presents itself. You can walk down its long and winding staircase or, better still, take the lift down to the beginning of the passageway which, completed in 1912, runs under the Thames and takes visitors 'south of the river'. It is an eerie, chilly walk along a seemingly infinite channel; and you wonder if the end is ever going to appear. Fortunately it does, and is well worth the effort when you catch a first glance of the massive, brown-bricked rear of the old Regal Cinema and then, to its right, the exquisite Odeon formation originated by George Coles. Both are neighbours along a part of Woolwich High Street, with Canary Wharf Tower being seen in the far distance. Advancing up the hill to John Wilson Street, past the Regal to your left, and over a zebra crossing, you arrive in front of the rolling curves of a peach-coloured Woolwich Coronet (*née* Odeon).

Woolwich Odeon

When you're a kid you think things will be the same forever . . .

Starting out in October 1937 with the *Gang Show*, the Odeon, its exterior coated in a buff mottled black with facing slabs, remains in a comely condition. It is a lovely curvaceous elevation that gently guides the eye along its smooth, cream-tiled faience frame, now faded in differing tones. In its heyday, the Woolwich Odeon on John Powis Street had neon strip lighting to flatter its already alluring external contours, with the ubiquitous Odeon name running along its side as it looks out to the Granada Cinema opposite. As an Odeon cinema, it shut its doors on 17 October 1981 with William Hurt starring in *The Janitor* (1981) as its final afternoon feature. A couple of years later, the flicks came back to life as the new Coronet Cinema premièred the third installment of the original *Star Wars* saga, *Return of the Jedi* (1983). Past modernisation back in 1964 had reduced the seating totality by some 700 or so but the last proprietor, Coronet Cinemas, has left their signage up outside the building with Screens 1 & 2 display boards still in place. *My Favourite Martian* (1999) would give the impression of being the final film projected on the second screen, as its poster remains as a reminder of the cinema's not-too-distant past. An 'All Enquiries' board hanging off its façade advises investors that the theatre is available for sale.

Two views of the Woolwich Odeon.

The Woolwich Granada

'The most romantic theatre ever built'

Five sets of double, glass-paned wooden doors take the enthusiast into the foyer of the Gala bingo club, situated at the beginning of Powis Street. It came to the end of its film exhibiting life way back in 1966, when bingo announced itself in October, and has been in residency since. Today, the recognisable blue and yellow livery of the Gala Bingo company veils the outside of the cinema, which still retains its two flag-poles, though now sadly no longer with the Union Jack flag billowing near to the commanding Thames breeze.

The one-time Granada Cinema is but a footstep away from the Odeon (also known as Coronet), with its vestibule entered through a further set of doors where a sensational vision awaits: from the dull, stoic town-hall like exterior, it is transformed into a chandelier-lined cavern. The sombre mood is relinquished with an Impressionistic instant. Devised by Komisarjevsky, the Gothic interior has an almost celestial atmosphere, defined in the opening celebratory brochure as 'The most romantic theatre ever built'. Defined by a selection of dark and mute-coloured figures, embellished by gild-edged frames, the view succinctly destroys the stiffness of the exterior architecture. Of course, this is the work of Cecil Masey (with R.H. Wren) and it would be flippant to simply dismiss it without due consideration. The most clearly commanding feature of his Woolwich façade is the high tower which does extract some interest as the structure crawls around Powis Street from its spot on corresponding John Wilson Street. A sense of anti-climax is experienced from seeing the exterior of this modern, streamlined Granada, particularly as it is inescapable not to contrast it with the vibrancy of the parallel George Coles Odeon building. The two picture houses are geographically close, yet far removed from one another in style.

The Woolwich Granada, now Gala Bingo.

The Regal Cinema

'We come along on Saturday morning greeting everybody with a smile.'
(Children's club song)

From the solid, green-topped peaks of the University of Greenwich building at the bottom of Wellington Street, the Regal Cinema now trades under the Galaxy entertainment name and, previously, was a nightclub venue called Flamingos. 'Galaxy: A new dawn in London's club life', proclaim the poster hoardings outside the main entrance of the old cinema, built on the site of the Woolwich Hippodrome. The actual boards look to have been there for quite some time, although it is questionable that they date back to the original cinema days. The British war picture *The Dambusters* was the first piece of celluloid to be projected onto the Regal screen on 19 September 1955; films ceased less than thirty years later with *Who Dares Wins* (1981) screening there in November 1982.

Situated next to the town hall, the Regal Cinema is small in comparison to the Odeon and Granada theatres sited a mere five minute walk away. Its façade has remained unaffected except for some metalwork attached presumably to give it a terraced impression atop of the entrance canopy. This aspect of its appearance is not authentic and is regrettably at odds with the prevailing aesthetic, marring an otherwise pleasant broad, brickworked face. Coated in green with magnolia on its lower brick structure continuing up to a height of the doorway leading into the club, the Regal has distinguishing window configurations that make it distinct. Two narrow, turret-shaped windows are set off by three further, centrally-situated windows of an equally condensed scale above the canopy.

The Regal Cinema, Woolwich.

There are other possible theatres scattered around the town centre, but I could not be absolutely certain in my estimations. A couple of buildings possessed the right shape and my inclination was to suspect them, at one point or another, of having been cinemas. What is absolutely evident is that Beresford Square, following on from Powis Street, home of an Iceland store, was where the lights of the Century Cinema once shone. This was a picture palace owned and controlled by the Granada circuit towards the end of its days in the late 1950s and early '60s. Memories may have been dimmed as time has marched relentlessly forth, but I was informed by a Woolwich resident and former trainee projectionist at the Century that both cinemas were owned by Granada Cinemas (the other being the Granada on Powis Street). Part of this man's responsibilities involved the weekly task of carrying newsreel film from the Granada to be shown at the Century, so it seems that its final years were not the most dignified, as were many cinemas. 'It [The Century] was dirty and really on its last legs', recounted another former cinema-goer, who had moved to the district back in early 1960s. Woolwich is an obscure kind of place, inevitably making a definition hard to establish; with its large, grand architecture subscribing to a past that feels as if it should be one of the Channel Islands: forever finding itself in a more genteel time.

Bibliography

Various sources of information and factual details have been generated from talking with innumerable individuals over the course of researching this project, as well as from visits to many local studies libraries. Listed below are the titles which proved to be very useful as starting points. Secondary sources have been acknowledged throughout the text. However, it has to be said that, occasionally, contradictions have occurred regarding various facts and figures and I would welcome corrections or additions. Special thanks to Kate Taylor of the Mercia Cinema Society for her invaluable help.

Atwell, David. *Cathedrals of the Movies: History of British Cinemas and Their Audiences*, Architectural Press, 1981

Eyles, Allen. *ABC: The First Name in Entertainment*, BFI Publishing, 1993

—*The Granada Theatres*, BFI Publishing, 1998

—*Gaumont: British Cinemas*, BFI Publishing, 1996

Field, Audrey. *Picture Palace: A Social History of the Cinema*, Gentry Books, 1973

Gray, Richard. *Cinemas in Britain: 100 Years of Cinema Architecture*, Lund Humphries, 1996

Grimwood, Bob. *The Cinemas of Essex*, Mercia Cinema Society, 1995

Hill, Susan. *Breaking Glass*, Star Books, 1980

Howes, J.W. & Law, D. *'Shopper's Paradise': A History of High Street, Walthamstow*, Walthamstow Historic Society, 1991

Morgan, Guy. *Red Roses Every Night – London Cinemas Under Fire*, Quality Press, 1948

Morton Shand, P. *The Architect of Pleasure: Modern Theatres & Cinemas*, London, 1930

Webb, Malcolm. *Gazetteer of Greater London's Suburban Cinemas 1946–86*, Amber Valley, 1986

Index of Cinemas

Apollo (Stoke Newington) 40
Avenue Cinema (Ealing) 1

Boleyn Electric Theatre/Odeon (East Ham) 112
Brixton Astoria Cinema 76
Bruce Grove Cinema 36

Canadian Cinema Theatre (Tottenham) 34
Carlton Cinema (Upton Park) 111
Coliseum Cinema (Haringey) 52
Coliseum (Stoke Newington) 40
Coronation Picture Palace (Manor Park) 108
Coronet Cinema (Notting Hill Gate) 65
Coronet Cinema (Turnpike Lane) 50

Dominion Cinema (Walthamstow) 100

Electric Cinema (Notting Hill) 61
Empire Cinema (Walthamstow) 102

Finsbury Park Astoria 13
Forum Cinema (Ealing) 9

Gate (Notting Hill Gate) 69
Gaumont Palace (Haringey) 53
Gaumont State Cinema (Kilburn) 17
Granada Cinema (East Ham) 113
Granada Cinema (Hoe Street) 103
Granada Tooting 87

Imperial Cinema (Tottenham) 38

Kensington Cinema 10

Maida Vale Picture House 22
Majestic Cinema (South Woodford) 25

Odeon Cinema (Forest Gate) 109
Odeon Swiss Cottage 73

Palace Cinema (Southall) 59
Palace Theatre (Tottenham) 34
Palladium (Brixton) 81
Plaza Cinema (Walthamstow) 92
Premier Electric Theatre (East Ham) 115
Premier Electric Theatre (Haringey) 56
Premier Electric Theatre (Walthamstow) 98
Pyke's Cinematograph Hall (Brixton) 82
Pyke's Shepherd's Bush Cinematograph Theatre 32

Queens Cinema (Bayswater) 69

Regal Cinema (Highams Park) 26
Regal Cinema (Woolwich) 119
Rio Cinema (Stoke Newington) 42
Ritz Cinema (Leyton) 106
Ritzy Cinema (Brixton) 79

St James Electric Theatre (Walthamstow) 97
Savoy Cinema (Leyton) 94
Savoy (Stoke Newington) 42
Shepherd's Bush Pavilion 30
Stratford Rex Cinema 84
Studios 5,6,7,8 (Bruce Grove) 37

Troxy Cinema (Stepney) 45

Vogue Cinema (Stoke Newington) 39

West Ealing Kinema (Ealing) 7
Woolwich Granada 118
Woolwich Odeon 117